The Complete Guide to

BENGAL CATS

Tarah Schwartz

Publication Data

Tarah Schwartz
The Complete Guide to Bengal Cats – First edition.
Summary: "Successfully raising a Bengal cat from kitten to old age"
Provided by publisher.
ISBN: 978-1-961846-04-3
[1. The Complete Guide to Bengal Cats – Non-Fiction] I. Title.

This book has been written with the published intent to provide accurate and authoritative information in regard to the subject matter included. While every reasonable precaution has been taken in preparation of this book the author and publisher expressly disclaim responsibility for any errors, omissions, or adverse effects arising from the use or application of the information contained inside. The techniques and suggestions are to be used at the reader's discretion and are not to be considered a substitute for professional veterinary care. If you suspect a medical problem with your cat, consult your veterinarian.

Design by Sorin Rădulescu
First paperback edition, 2023

TABLE OF CONTENTS

Chapter 1

Chapter 2

Chapter 3

Chapter 13

Into the World of Showing

Chapter 14

Your Aging Bengal Cat

Chapter 15

When It's Time to Say Goodbye

CHAPTER 1

What is a Bengal Cat?

Physical Characteristics

> *Bengal cats do best in a large home that has plenty of room for them to run, jump, and play. They like to be where the action is and they get bored easily. Bengal cats are good with kids. I know this for a fact because I have two kids. I raise Bengals because that is the type of pet I want in my home with my kids. However, I usually do not recommend Bengal kittens for families with children under the age of four unless they have previous cat/kitten experience. Bengal kittens play hard, and very young children could get scratched and bitten. Bengals are a lot of fun to spend time with. They are smart, loving, and adventurous.*
>
> ERIN H.
>
> *Sarasota Bengals*

Bengal cats are one of the most unique and striking breeds of domestic cats. They are a medium- to large-sized breed that has a muscular and athletic build. Bengals have a distinctive wild appearance that stems from their ancestor, the Asian leopard cat, a wildcat native to Southeast Asia. Their coats have a beautiful, luxurious texture and are covered in a variety of eye-catching colors, including brown, silver, snow, and charcoal.

One of the most striking features of Bengal cats is their coat pattern. The cats have coats that are covered in spots and rosettes, giving them

Photo Courtesy of Jennifer Gray

a look similar to that of a miniature leopard or jaguar. The spots and rosettes are arranged randomly across their coats, making each Bengal cat unique. The pattern of their coats changes with age and becomes more pronounced as they mature. Many Bengals also have "glitter," which is a unique and distinctive shine to their coats.

In addition to their signature coats, Bengal cats have large, expressive eyes. The eyes are usually green or gold, though some snow-colored Bengals may have blue eyes. Their eyes are set at a slight angle, giving them a more alert and wild appearance than many domestic breeds. Their ears are large and pointed, giving them an alert and curious expression.

The body shape of a Bengal cat is also distinctive. They have long, muscular bodies with broad chests and powerful legs. Their back legs are slightly longer than their front legs, giving them a pronounced slope to their back. They have broad, rounded heads with strong jawlines and short, thick necks.

Bengal cats are a beautiful breed with a distinctive exotic appearance. The luxurious coats, unique coat patterns, large expressive eyes, and athletic bodies make them one of the most captivating breeds of domestic cats.

Temperament and Behavior

> "
> The ideal home for a Bengal cat is one that can embrace an active and curious personality. Bengals are known for enjoying the company of their owners and do best with another active cat to play with.
>
> JESSICA PETRAS
> *Liberty Bengals*
> "

Although Bengals are most well known for their appearance, true Bengal lovers know that the breed's best feature is its personality. Bengal cats are known for their playful, energetic, and curious personalities. They have a natural instinct to explore their environment and will often spend hours playing with toys or investigating their surroundings. They are intelligent cats that require plenty of mental stimulation to keep them happy and healthy.

Despite their wild appearance, Bengal cats are generally affectionate and social cats. They enjoy spending time with their owners and will often follow them around the house. If you enjoy spending time alone, a Bengal may not be the right breed for you. The breed is known for its love of water. Many Bengals will play in water bowls or try to jump in the shower with their owners.

Bengal cats are highly trainable and can be taught a variety of tricks and behaviors. They are known for their love of climbing and jumping, and many owners will create custom climbing structures or perches for their Bengal cats to play on. Bengals are also very active and require plenty of exercise, so owners should be prepared to provide them with plenty of toys and playtime.

Like all cats, Bengals are independent and may prefer to have their own space to retreat to when they want some alone time. However, they are generally quite social and thrive on attention and interaction with their owners. Bengals are also known for their vocalizations and will often meow or purr to communicate with their owners.

It's important to note that socialization is a contributing factor to any Bengal's temperament. A well-socialized Bengal will always make a better companion than a cat that has not been exposed to a wide range of experiences. Additionally, cats are individuals, and although the breed is known for certain personality traits, it's possible that not all Bengals will fit the same description.

Photo Courtesy of Jessica Black

Caring for a High-Energy Cat

> *A home that understands these cats truly attach to their owners and can have a higher energy level is very important. I look for a home that has planned energy outlets for their new Bengal and which is ready for a cat that wants to 'talk' to them, interact with them, and be an active member of their day-to-day family activities.*
>
> RENEE RORAGEN
> *The Rhine Bengals*

Bengals are active, high-energy cats that need daily physical and mental exercise. If you haven't owned a high-energy cat before, be prepared to spend time entertaining your new cat each day. Keeping your Bengal entertained is crucial to keeping him out of trouble, but it's also an important aspect of his overall health and well-being. Entertaining your Bengal shouldn't be a chore but rather a fun bonding experience.

It's not always easy to come home after a long day at work to a cat that's bouncing off the walls. There are many ways you can keep a high-energy cat entertained while you're gone, but you'll also want to spend time each day actively interacting with your Bengal. If this sounds like a lot of work, it is, but most Bengal owners find it worth the effort. If you are able to have more than one cat in your home, you may find that the cats are able to better entertain themselves when they have a playmate.

Providing your Bengal with an enriching environment is key to keeping him entertained, whether you are home or not. Elevated surfaces and hiding places, such as those provided by cat trees or shelves, are essential. Bengals love to climb and view their world from above, so be sure to give your Bengal as many options as possible. Cat furniture should always be sturdy so that it can withstand an energetic and playful Bengal.

Interactive toys are another great option for keeping your Bengal busy. Battery-powered toys that move around on their own can be fun,

Photo Courtesy of
Lisa Ferrigno

but many cats will get bored after a few minutes. It can be helpful to have a variety of toys on hand so that you can swap them out when your cat needs something new. Puzzle feeders are also a fun way to entertain a busy Bengal. You can use your cat's daily meals or a few tasty treats. The puzzle feeder makes your cat work for his food, which helps to keep his mind engaged and encourages instinctual feeding behavior.

Providing an indoor-only cat with a taste of the outdoors can also provide plenty of physical and mental stimulation. If you have an outdoor space, you may want to consider building a "catio" or enclosed space that your cat can access. By keeping the space enclosed, your Bengal will stay safe but will still get to see, smell, and feel the natural environment. If you are unable to build an enclosed outdoor space, you can also set up a bird feeder outside your cat's favorite window. Many cats will spend hours watching the birds each day.

One-on-one time is important for your Bengal's overall well-being. Be sure to spend time each day playing with him and giving him your full attention. You can try using a wand toy or piece of string to encourage your cat to exercise, or you can teach your Bengal how to play fetch. This focused playtime can sometimes feel like a chore, but it's important to remember that you are your cat's entire world, so it's important to do your best to give him the best life possible.

Is a Bengal Cat Right for You?

> **"**
>
> *Bengals are best suited for an active family, but not an overly busy one. It's important to have enough time to spend playing with the cat or at least providing some individual attention. If a family is too busy with a lot of activities outside the home, the cat is often left to entertain itself or sit alone being bored for many hours.*
>
> ELIZABETH NOLTE
> *Southern Pines Bengals*
>
> **"**

Bengals are a stunning and exotic breed, and many people fall in love at first sight. However, they are not the ideal breed for everyone, so it's important to consider whether they are the right cat for you and your lifestyle. Any cat is a huge responsibility, but Bengals, in particular, require a lot of attention. It's important to consider whether you're ready for this commitment before you sign the adoption agreement.

FUN FACT
Breed Recognition

Bengal cats were recognized as an experimental domestic cat breed by the International Cat Association (TICA) in 1983 and given full recognition in 1993. The Cat Fanciers' Association (CFA) officially recognized this breed in 2016. Today, most major international cat associations, including the Canadian Cat Association, the American Cat Fanciers Association, and the Governing Council of the Cat Fancy, now recognize Bengal cats.

Bengals are friendly and outgoing cats, but they can be demanding. Attention-seeking behavior is common, especially with cats that do not have an enriching environment. If you are unwilling to provide your cat with entertainment each day and do not like having a cat that follows you from room to room, you may need to consider another breed. Bengals are not a breed that you can leave alone for long periods of time.

You should also consider whether you can afford the

Photo Courtesy of
Bella Sera

expenses of cat ownership. Although many supplies will be a one-time purchase, you will need to budget for the regular cost of food and litter. Routine veterinary care can also be expensive, but you will need to make sure you can afford emergency care as well. Additionally, purebred cats are not inexpensive to purchase. The price you pay for a well-bred Bengal will depend on many factors, but you can expect to pay much more than you would for a plain domestic cat.

Sharing your life with a Bengal is a rewarding experience, but it can be a lot of work. Welcoming a new pet into your home should never be an impulsive decision, especially if you have multiple family members sharing your home. It's crucial that each member of your household is on the same page when it comes to pet ownership. Once you've thoroughly considered your options, you can make the decision together as a family.

CHAPTER 2

History of the Bengal Cat

The Wild Origins of the Bengal

Though the earliest records of Asian leopard cats being bred with domestic cats date to the late 1800s, it wasn't until the 1960s that efforts were made to create a new breed. The modern Bengal was originally developed by Jean Mill of California, who crossed a domestic cat with an Asian leopard cat, which is a small wild feline found throughout Southeast Asia.

In the 1950s, geneticist Willard Centerwall had a breeding program of his own at Loma Linda University. Though the purpose of the program was genetic testing, some of the cats used in the program went on to be used in Mill's breeding program. Thanks to Mill's efforts over the next decade, the Bengal breed began to take shape. The goal was to create a hybrid breed with the exotic looks of a wild cat but the personality and temperament of a domestic one. This new breed was named the Bengal after the scientific name of the Asian leopard cat, *Prionailurus bengalensis.*

In the early years of the breed's development, Mill crossed the Asian leopard cat with various domestic cats, including Siamese, Burmese, and Egyptian Mau breeds. However, it wasn't until she discovered a male domestic cat with a distinctive coat pattern reminiscent of the Asian leopard cat's that she was able to create the Bengal breed's signature look. Mill then bred this male with a female Asian leopard cat to produce the first generation of Bengals.

Photo Courtesy of Eileen Provins

The Bengal breed began to gain popularity in the 1980s, but it wasn't until 1991 that it was officially recognized by The International Cat Association (TICA). TICA was the first organization to recognize the Bengal as a distinct breed. Other cat associations, including the Cat Fanciers Association (CFA), followed suit and recognized the Bengal as a breed in the early 2000s.

Hybrid Cats

Hybrid cats are the result of breeding a wild cat species with a domestic cat. Typically, the goal of these breedings is to produce a cat with the appearance of a wild cat but the temperament of a domestic cat. However, hybrids can be controversial due to concerns over their welfare, the potential for aggression, and legality of ownership. The legal restrictions of hybrid cat ownership will be discussed toward the end of this chapter.

Photo Courtesy of
Keith Uptain

Bengal cats are one of the most well-known hybrid cat breeds, resulting from the breeding of an Asian leopard cat with a domestic cat. The first three filial generations of the Bengals are considered the foundation of the breed. It should be noted that the terms F1, F2, and F3 are not the correct genetic terms for these early generations but have been used incorrectly for so many years that it is now standard to refer to them as such. It is also common for early-generation male Bengals to be infertile, so only the females are bred.

HELPFUL TIP
What Does F1 Mean?

Domestic Bengal cats are categorized based on how many generations removed they are from their wild Asian leopard ancestor. For example, the offspring of a wild Asian leopard and a domestic cat is called an F1 Bengal cat. The next generation would be considered F2, and so on. According to TICA, a Bengal cat must be at least an F4 to be registered. (TICA does not recognize F1–F3 Bengal cats as domestic breeds.)

The earliest generation of Bengals are known as F1 Bengal cats, which are 50% wild cat and 50% domestic cat. F1 Bengals are often larger and more active than domestic cats and can have a more pronounced wild temperament. They also require more socialization and training than domestic cats and are not recommended for first-time cat owners.

The offspring of an F1 Bengal cat and a domestic cat are known as F2 Bengals, which are 25% wild cat and 75% domestic cat. F2 Bengals tend to be more social and easier to handle than F1s, but they still have a higher activity level than most domestic cats.

The offspring of an F2 Bengal cat and a domestic cat are known as F3 Bengals, which are 12.5% wild cat and 87.5% domestic cat. F3 Bengals tend to have a more docile temperament than F1 or F2 Bengals and are usually easier to handle.

Today, most Bengal cats have many generations of distance from their wild ancestors, but a few breeders continue using Asian leopard cats in their breeding programs. It's important to note that early-generation Bengals are recognized by most cat registries but are not eligible to be shown. As discussed later in the chapter, there are also legal restrictions concerning the ownership of these hybrids in some areas.

The Modern Bengal Cat

> *As far as the difference between a Bengal and a regular domestic house cat, the biggest difference is the intelligence of the Bengal. Bengals can open drawers where they know their favorite treat is hiding!! They love to touch the running stream of water while you are brushing your teeth. They are a verbal breed and will tell you what they want or need, and after spending enough time with your Bengal, you will understand what it is telling you.*
>
> TIFFANI THIEL
> *Baby Bengals OC*

Photo Courtesy of Drew Spangler

> "
>
> *I honestly don't think Bengals are too much different from the average cat. Bengals are known for being more adventurous and rambunctious, but I'm going to guess that comes more from your F1 or F2 types. Most Bengals are now removed enough from the wild and are more like the average domestic cat.*
>
> RHEA SCHMITT
> *Bella Luna Gatte*
>
> "

Today, the Bengal cat is one of the most popular breeds in the world. Thanks to decades of selective breeding, the breed's stunning appearance and affectionate personality have stolen the hearts of families all over the globe. It's a beloved breed that continues to captivate cat lovers with its wild looks and domestic nature.

Despite their popularity, Bengal cats are not without their controversies. Some animal welfare organizations have raised concerns about the breeding practices used to produce the Bengal cat breed, particularly those involving hybridization with wild cat species. It is important for potential owners to thoroughly research breeders and ensure that they are operating ethically and responsibly before acquiring a Bengal cat.

Legal Restrictions

While F1, F2, and F3 Bengal cats are recognized by some cat registries, they are not legal to own in all areas. Some states or countries have restrictions on owning hybrid cats, so potential owners should check their local regulations before bringing one home. Additionally, it is important for potential owners to research the breed and ensure they are prepared for the unique needs and behaviors of early-generation hybrid cats before adopting one.

The legal restrictions on owning hybrid cats, such as the Bengal, vary depending on the state or country. In some places, hybrid cats of any generation are completely legal to own, while in others, they may be prohibited or require a special permit. It is important for potential owners

Photo Courtesy of
Jennifer Gray

to research the laws in their area before acquiring a hybrid cat to avoid any legal issues.

In the United States, some states prohibit the ownership of hybrid cats altogether, while others may require permits or have restrictions based on the generation of the hybrid. For example, in New York, it is illegal to own a Bengal cat or any other hybrid cat that is more than 25% wild cat. In California, hybrid cats are legal to own, but only if they are at least four generations removed from the wild cat ancestor.

Outside of the United States, laws regarding the ownership of hybrid cats can vary widely. In the United Kingdom, for example, it is illegal to own a hybrid cat that is more than 50% wild cat. In Australia, hybrid cats are generally prohibited from importation, and the laws regarding ownership vary by state.

It is important for potential owners to thoroughly research the laws in their area before acquiring a hybrid cat. In addition to legal considerations, potential owners should also be aware of the unique needs and behaviors of hybrid cats and ensure they are prepared to provide the proper care and attention. Hybrid cats can make wonderful pets, but they require a dedicated and knowledgeable owner to ensure their health and happiness.

CHAPTER 3

Purchasing a Bengal Cat

"
Bengals are a great fit for a home wanting companionship with an interactive pet. Bengals keep an energetic, curious, and interactive personality for life. They love the playfulness of children and are not intimidated. Bengals love the companionship of cat-friendly dogs as much or more than other cats. If you are away from home a lot, it is good to have another animal for them to socialize with and form companionship. Bengals in my experience have been a delight for children needing companionship or that have allergies.

PENNY T. LILLY
Silverlilly's Bengals
"

Buying vs. Adopting

After you've decided that a Bengal cat is the right breed for you and your family, you'll need to decide whether you would prefer to buy your Bengal from a reputable breeder or rescue organization. Each option has its pros and cons, so you'll need to consider your choice carefully. At this stage, you should not only think about a preferred gender but also whether you prefer a kitten or an adult. If you have any interest in showing or breeding your Bengal, you'll also want to decide now.

In general, kittens tend to be more work than adult cats. You will need to spend more time on training and socialization with a kitten, as well as spending more money on routine veterinary care. If you are not interested in the additional cost and work, an adult cat may be best. Kittens and adult cats are often available from both breeders and rescue organizations, but knowing which you prefer can help narrow down your search. When deciding on the age of your new cat, you should also consider any existing pets in your home. Bengals are high-energy cats, and a rambunctious kitten may be overwhelming for older pets. However, if your existing pets are young and energetic, a Bengal kitten may be fine.

When deciding whether you are interested in purchasing your Bengal from a breeder or a rescue organization, you must consider whether you would like to show your new cat. If you want to get involved in cat shows or would potentially like to breed your Bengal, you will want to work with a reputable breeder. You will not be able to find a show- or breeding-quality Bengal at a rescue organization or shelter. Be aware that buying a pure-bred cat from a reputable breeder will not be an inexpensive endeavor, especially if you're searching for one of outstanding quality.

If you are not interested in showing or breeding and are solely looking for a companion animal, either a breeder or rescue will be able to provide you with what you're looking for. There are pros and cons to both choices, so you will need to decide what's important to you. Imagine your perfect Bengal and decide where you are most likely to find him. Most reputable breeders will provide kitten owners with lifelong support and guidance, but again, you can expect to pay upward of $1,000 for your new cat. Some breeders price adult cats lower than kittens, but this is not always the case. Adoption fees at a rescue or shelter are likely to be far cheaper, but it can be difficult to find a purebred Bengal.

HELPFUL TIP
Bengal Rescue

Bengal rescues play a crucial role in providing a second chance to Bengal cats in need of homes. One such rescue, Bengal Rescue, was established in 2020 and strives to find homes for Bengal and hybrid cats. With the help of volunteers, Bengal Rescue has launched a nationwide network of foster homes where Bengal cats can await proper veterinary care and forever-home placement without the stress of a shelter. For more information about Bengal Rescue, visit www.bengalrescue.org.

Additionally, cats from rescue organizations are generally already spayed or neutered and have been given all necessary vaccines and medical care. If your Bengal comes from a breeder, you may be responsible for some or all of the costs associated with these procedures. However, Bengals from breeders typically come with a health guarantee, so you will likely have an overall healthier cat.

Be aware that Bengals are an in-demand breed, so you may face a waiting period before you are able to find the right cat. Many ethical breeders have waitlists of up to a year or longer. Even rescue organizations can take time to review and approve potential adopters, so don't get impatient. It may be easier to buy a Bengal from a local backyard breeder, but you will not be getting the same quality as you would with a reputable breeder. Instead, you should start your search long before you're ready to welcome a new cat into your home so that you can find the right person or people to work with.

Pet stores and backyard breeders often have purebred cats on demand, but purchasing from them is not recommended. They do not value the breed as a whole and only view the cats as a means to pad their wallet. Unethical breeders and kitten mills do not perform health tests on their cats prior to breeding, which can result in unhealthy kittens. Although Bengals are known for their friendly temperaments, when quality is not a priority, you can end up with Bengals that are fearful or aggressive. Additionally, they may not even resemble a purebred Bengal once they reach adulthood. If you are truly interested in finding the Bengal cat of your dreams, have the patience to find the right breeder or rescue rather than supporting greedy and unethical individuals.

Rescues and Shelters

Although many pet owners are aware that there are good and bad breeders, it's important to understand that not all rescue organizations are ethical. Many prioritize their income over the welfare of the animals in their care. It's important to do your research and have a clear idea of what you're looking for. Some unethical rescues may charge outrageous fees for purebred cats or cats that look like they could be purebred. Without a pedigree, it can be difficult to determine if a cat is purebred, and some rescues may try to pass off a mixed-breed cat as a Bengal. Though it's unlikely that a cat will have rosettes without a Bengal heritage, they may claim that an unusual coat pattern makes the cat a Bengal.

*Photo Courtesy of
Melissa Johnson*

HELPFUL TIP
How Much Do They Cost?

The average price of Bengal cats can vary depending on age, lineage, coat quality, and breeder reputation. Bengal kittens typically range from around $1,000 to $2,500 or more. In contrast, adult Bengal cats may be available at a lower cost, depending on individual circumstances.

Though these cats also deserve a loving home, you may be overpaying for a cat that does not have the Bengal's signature looks and temperament.

Thankfully, the internet has made it easier than ever to spot the red flags of an unethical rescue. Past adopters with bad experiences may leave bad reviews on search engines or comments on social media. Be sure to look up the organization before contacting them about an adoption application.

If you are interested in adopting a Bengal from a rescue organization, it's best to search for a breed-specific rescue. Bengals are a popular breed, and some people get them without realizing that they may not be the right cat for their lifestyle, so it is possible to find purebred Bengals in rescue. A breed-specific rescue will have more knowledge about the Bengal breed and will be better able to match you to the right cat than an all-breed rescue. They are also more likely to be able to tell a purebred Bengal from a lookalike and will likely charge an appropriate adoption fee based on the cat's age and care level while in rescue. They may also be in contact with other rescues across the country and may be able to search their network for your dream Bengal.

If a rescue does not have the exact cat you're looking for, it may still be worth your time to contact them and fill out an adoption application. As previously mentioned, it can take time to be approved for adoption as most rescues are volunteer-run organizations. Once you are approved, you will already have an application on file when your ideal Bengal comes into rescue.

It's important to be aware that if you live in a rural area, it can be difficult to find a purebred Bengal in rescue nearby. You may need to search in another area or even out of state to find the right cat. Some rescues are hesitant to work with potential adopters in another state, so be sure to ask before filling out an application. Additionally, some rescues may work with volunteers and other organizations to arrange transport for the animals in their care, so you may also want to ask about options if the rescue is far from home.

Photo Courtesy of Sabrina Lawson

As mentioned earlier in the chapter, it will probably be less expensive to rescue a Bengal, but most organizations do charge more for purebred cats. Many organizations charge between $100 and $300, but some may charge more. Kittens are also typically more expensive to adopt than adult cats simply because they require more veterinary care. It's common for senior cats to have lower fees, as they are often overlooked by potential adopters. If you are just interested in a companion animal, you may want to consider taking in an older cat. It can be incredibly rewarding to give a senior Bengal the love and affection he deserves in his golden years.

Tips for Adoption

> *It is important to find out from a rescue organization if the cat has been abandoned due to the fact that it has been neglected, not socialized, or treated poorly. Bengals can lose their trust and or never learn to bond with people and will not aim to please like a Bengal who has been loved. If a Bengal is just very shy from lack of socialization, it can still make a nice pet and you can give the cat a good life by getting it accustomed to your presence over time. However, it may never come to sit with you.*
>
> PENNY T. LILLY
> *Silverlilly's Bengals*

Although Bengals are known for their appearance, it's important not to prioritize looks over temperament. You may have a certain color in mind, but the Bengal of your dreams may look a little different, so it's important to be open-minded.

Many rescue organizations work with foster homes so that the cats don't have to live in a kennel environment. The benefit of this arrangement is that the foster homes will generally have a good idea of the cat's temperament and personality, especially if it has been in their care for some time. If the cat is new to rescue, it's common for them to be nervous in new situations and around new people. The cat you meet at first glance may not be the same cat known by the foster home. It can take time for some cats to warm up to new people, so it's important to ask questions about the cat's behavior and preferences.

You may want to ask questions about

- Eating habits
- Food preferences
- Behavior toward other cats
- Behavior toward children
- Behavior toward dogs or other pets
- Litter box habits
- Play habits
- Activity level
- How vocal the cat may be
- Any bad habits the cat may have
- Overall health
- Vaccination status
- Whether the cat has been spayed or neutered

Remember, it's important to be honest with rescue volunteers. If you've found your ideal Bengal, but he doesn't like kids, it would not be fair to be dishonest about bringing him home to a house full of children. Again, it can take time to find the right Bengal for your lifestyle, so be sure to ask plenty of questions to make sure it's a good match.

In general, it's recommended to spend at least 30 minutes with any cat that you are interested in adopting. Many shelters have visitation rooms, and many foster homes will allow you to settle in and get to know the cat. Try not to reach out and touch a timid cat, as it may react out of fear. Instead, wait for him to approach you. Never pick up a cat that you don't know. If the cat is a typical confident and outgoing Bengal, it shouldn't take long for him to warm up to you. You can try playing with a

Photo Courtesy of
Carrie Adams

wand or string toy to engage the cat and evaluate his energy level. Once the cat is more comfortable with you, you can try inviting him onto your lap for petting.

Remember, it can take several weeks or more for a cat's true personality to come out in a new home. Typically, the longer that the cat has been in rescue, the longer it will take for him to fully decompress. The first few weeks with your Bengal will be discussed later in the book, but don't be concerned if your new cat is a bit more nervous or shy than you expected once he arrives home.

CHAPTER 4

All About Bengal Breeders

Finding a Breeder

> "
>
> *When you are looking for a Bengal cat, I recommend you talk to the breeder. Tell them what your home is like so they can match you up with the perfect cat. Also, look at their website and other social media content. They should be able to share pictures and videos of their cats and kittens. They should be willing to do a video chat so you can see the kitten. A good breeder will take the time to talk to you and answer any questions you might have. A reputable breeder and their cats will be registered with TICA or CFA. They will do genetic testing on their cats to ensure that they do not have any hereditary diseases, such as PK deficiency and progressive retinal atrophy (PRA).*
>
> ERIN H.
> *Sarasota Bengals*
>
> "

When searching for a reputable Bengal breeder, a good place to start is with your preferred cat association's website. A few of the main cat associations are the Cat Fanciers Association (CFA), Cat Fanciers' Federation (CFF), and The International Cat Association (TICA). These organizations usually have a list of registered breeders of all recognized cat breeds published on their websites. Breed-specific

Photo Courtesy of Tammy Smith

organizations such as The International Bengal Cat Society (TIBCS) are also great resources.

To avoid unethical breeders, it's best not to start your search on classified ad websites, as few reputable breeders would choose to advertise there. You should also avoid any breeder that is not registered with a cat association, as they will be unable to provide pedigrees for their kittens. Although pedigrees do not seem important for the average pet cat, they are proof that your Bengal is, indeed, a purebred Bengal. Without a pedigree, it will be impossible to prove that you are paying for a purebred cat.

Once you've located one or more breeders in your desired area, it's time to do some research. The most important part of finding a good breeder is to locate proof of health testing. Ethical breeders typically post this information on their websites to make it easier for potential kitten buyers. However, some may only provide proof of testing upon request. If a breeder does not provide proof of health testing or claims that the cats are healthy because their vet says so, you are likely talking to a backyard breeder. Ethical breeders have nothing to hide and are happy to provide proof of all health tests.

As you examine the breeder's website, you'll also want to see how many cats they have

HEALTH ALERT
Sterile Males

Did you know that F1 to F3 male Bengal cats are sterile and cannot produce kittens? Sometimes even F4 males are sterile as well. Therefore, only female F1 through F3 cats are capable of reproduction, while Toms are not. This male infertility is likely due to genetics, though it isn't clear why F1 to F3 females are not sterile.

and how many litters they have at one time. Ethical breeders do not typically breed on a large scale and rarely have more than one or two litters available at a time. Breeders who produce a large number of kittens are considered kitten mills and are not reputable. When breeders produce so many litters at once, you can be sure that each kitten is not receiving the appropriate amount of care and attention.

Additionally, you should search for a Bengal breeder that adheres to the breed standard. The Bengal breed standard will be discussed in a later chapter, but essentially its purpose is to maintain a certain quality in the breed. This does not mean that every kitten a breeder produces will be perfect. Even two champion Bengals will not have an entire litter of show-quality kittens. However, it helps to ensure that those kittens and any future litters they may produce will resemble the Bengal as we know it.

After you've completed your screening and are ready to reach out to a breeder, be aware that you will probably undergo a bit of screening as well. The breeder will want to know some details about your home, family, and lifestyle so that they can match you to the right kitten. You may be asked questions about past or current pet ownership, years of cat experience, your typical schedule, and more. You may also be asked if you intend to keep your Bengal indoors or if you will allow him outdoor access. Even if the questions feel a bit intrusive at times, understand that the breeder is simply looking out for their beloved kittens. They want to make sure they go to homes where they are properly loved and cared for.

TIPS

For choosing the right Bengal Breeder
by Rhea Schmitt – Bella Luna Gatte

1 **Get to know your breeder!** A good breeder is more than happy to talk with you and answer any questions you have before, during, and long after the purchase of your Bengal!

2 **Learn the breeder's plan to make sure the kittens are raised to be well socialized.** Proper socialization is very important to having a Bengal with a good temperament. Ideally, the Bengals will be raised right in the family's home, so the kittens are well adapted to all the sights, sounds, smells, touches, etc., of home life when they go to their new homes. Kittens that are raised in a separate breeding facility or only a small room in the house will have a much harder time adapting to a new home.

3 **DNA testing on the breeding parents is a must in this day and age.** It's simple, cheap, and easy. If a breeder can't be bothered with this simple process to screen for genetic defects, then find someone else.

4 **Be very wary of scam breeders out there!** The internet and Facebook are ripe with scammers who show off cute pictures, take your money, and never give you a Bengal. Other times you get a cat that looks a bit like a Bengal but is not a purebred. Serious breeders will likely have an up-to-date website and a Facebook page with a lengthy history. Be aware of a page that was just started with limited information. New breeders do need to start somewhere, but they will work hard to establish a credible page.

Health Tests and Certifications

> *There are various classes of breeders, and it is imperative that potential owners support reputable, ethical breeders. It is important to find one that, at a minimum, genetically tests for PRA-b (Bengal blindness), PK-Deficiency (hemolytic anemia), and HCM (hypertrophic cardiomyopathy). An ideal breeder will be extremely dedicated, show their cats in TICA or CFA, have extensive knowledge of additional health testing, treatments, and have expertise in the ideal breed standard. When researching breeders, they should be able to provide you with a copy of each parent's genetic testing. This genetic test is usually completed by UC Davis or Optimal Selection. For HCM, it must be done by a cardiologist by echocardiogram prior to breeding and then have continued yearly to biyearly reevaluations.*
>
> JESSICA PETRAS
> *Liberty Bengals*

As mentioned earlier in the chapter, health testing is an important part of any ethical breeding program. All cats should be tested prior to breeding to make sure that they will not pass down any genetic diseases or conditions. Although this doesn't mean that it's impossible for a future kitten to have health problems, it helps improve the overall chances of a healthy life. Some breeds are more prone to specific health problems, and testing can help to reduce or even eliminate the problem from the gene pool.

At a minimum, an ethical Bengal breeder should test their breeding stock for hypertrophic cardiomyopathy (HCM) and polycystic kidney disease (PKD). It's also a good idea to test for progressive retinal atrophy (PRA), feline leukemia virus, and feline immunodeficiency virus.

HCM can affect any cat, whether purebred or mixed breed. The disease causes the heart's walls to thicken, decreasing its ability to pump blood efficiently. HCM is more prevalent in some breeds, including Bengals. Genetic testing can determine which cats are at a higher risk of developing the disorder, but the disease must be formally diagnosed with an echocardiogram. HCM is manageable with medication and life-style changes but cannot be cured.

PKD tends to be more prevalent in breeds with Persian ancestry, but it can occur in all breeds. The disease causes cysts to form inside the kidneys, which grow larger as the cat ages. Many cats with PKD have cysts present in their kidneys at birth, though many will develop cysts as they age. Eventually, the cysts damage the kidneys enough to cause kidney failure. Genetic testing can determine whether a cat has the defective gene PKD1, which causes the disease. As with HCM, cats affected with PKD can be managed but not cured.

PRA is a disease of the eye that results in degeneration of the retina. An affected cat's eyesight will deteriorate over time, eventually resulting in total blindness. The age at which a cat begins to show symptoms will depend on which form of the disease it is affected by. Early onset PRA is typically inherited, and most cats will be formally diagnosed by the time they are two to three months of age. Late-onset PRA doesn't typically appear until between two and five years of age. Genetic testing can reveal whether an individual cat has the affected gene. Deterioration of the retina can be slowed with treatment but not stopped, so affected cats will eventually lose their eyesight.

Feline leukemia virus, or FeLV, is a common disease that can affect any cat. It's believed that between 2 and 3 percent of all cats in the US are infected with the disease. FeLV is caused by a retrovirus, which weakens the immune system and puts the cat at risk for contracting other serious or fatal diseases. The virus is spread from cat to cat through nasal secretions and saliva. Feline immunodeficiency virus, or FIV, is also a common viral disease. It's estimated that up to 4 percent of all cats in the United States are infected with FIV. As the name suggests, the disease is similar to human immunodeficiency virus (HIV). Like HIV, it weakens the immune system and is incurable. Without treatment, cats affected by FIV may develop feline AIDS, or acquired immunodeficiency syndrome, which is often fatal. Although similar in effect, feline AIDS and FIV cannot be passed on to humans or other species. Since these diseases are not genetic, it's recommended that all cats be tested each time before they are bred to avoid passing the viruses on.

Reputable breeders that health test their breeding Bengals will typically offer a genetic health guarantee. The length of the guarantee will vary by each breeder's contract, but they are often good for two or three years. This guarantee means that if your kitten develops a genetic disease during this time, the breeder is obliged to take action. Depending on the contract, this may mean a replacement kitten or a refund.

> 66
>
> *A reputable breeder will do DNA testing for Bengal genetic diseases so they get the healthiest kittens, as well as parents. Kittens need to go home with a one-year health guarantee, all shots, microchip, deworming, registration papers, two vet checks, a spay/neuter contract, and a lifetime of advice from the breeder. A reputable breeder will keep in contact with their clients to make sure their cats are happy and healthy. To avoid scammers, a person looking for a Bengal cat should make sure the breeder has a website, is active on social media sites, and actually talk to a real person several times. Breeders should also be willing to allow clients to come to their cattery to see the kitten's parents. Also, most reputable breeders are on the TICA website.*
>
> SHEILA WHEATLEY
> *Wonder Spots Bengals*
>
> 99

Breeder Contracts and Guarantees

When you buy a purebred Bengal from a reputable breeder, you will likely be required to sign a contract before you are allowed to take possession of your new cat. Breeders' contracts are legally binding, so it's crucial that you spend time reading through it before you sign. If the idea of a contract intimidates you, understand that its purpose is to prioritize the health and well-being of the kitten. However, the document also protects both you and the breeder by stating your responsibilities should any problems arise. There is no standard contract used by breeders, so

Photo Courtesy of Julie Filion

it's important to read the document thoroughly to make sure you understand what you are agreeing to.

Many contracts include clauses about what veterinary care is required. The breeder may require buyers to agree not to declaw their Bengals due to the physical and emotional trauma of the procedure. If the cat is unaltered, the contract may state at which age, if at all, the cat should be spayed or neutered. Additionally, you may need to agree to keep the cat current on all routine care, such as vaccinations, deworming, and dental care.

If the breeder is offering a health guarantee, the contract will also describe what may be covered and for how long. Long-term guarantees typically cover genetic conditions, while short-term guarantees cover the overall health of the kitten at the moment you take possession. Some contracts will also state whether you need to take the kitten to your vet or quarantine him away from other animals within the first few days.

Many breeders' contracts discuss what should happen if you are no longer able to care for the cat. Typically, it will be required that you return the cat to the breeder or at least inform the breeder of rehoming. This is to prevent the cat from simply being dropped off at the local animal shelter. Many breeders would prefer to stay in contact with the new owners rather than losing track of the cat entirely.

As you read the contract, if you see anything you don't agree with, be sure to mention it to the breeder prior to signing. If you do not agree with something and break the terms of the contract, the breeder could potentially take legal action. Most breeders are happy to discuss their contract with any buyer to ensure that you are on the same page and avoid any legal issues.

> *Rather than just buying the first Bengal kitten you find available, it is better to choose the right breeder first and then wait for the right kitten. A good Bengal breeder will be genetically testing their breeding cats so that they do not produce offspring with common genetic defects, which could shorten or harm their quality of life. A good breeder breeds for good temperament as well as health and good breed traits. They will provide a written health guarantee and stand behind it in the event that something does go wrong. There are many Bengal breed groups on social media where you can meet other Bengal owners and talk to other owners about their experiences to find the right breeder fit for you.*
>
> TRACY WILSON
> *Wildtrax*

Choosing Your Perfect Kitten

> *Observe the temperament of the kitten and its parents. A well-socialized Bengal kitten should be curious, friendly, and comfortable with human interaction. Avoid kittens that display excessive fear or aggression. Consider the activity level that matches your family's lifestyle. Some Bengal kittens may be more active and require extra playtime and stimulation, while others may be more laid-back. Discuss with the breeder or rescue organization to find a suitable match. Also remember that Bengal kittens will change color as they grow older, so make sure you tell the breeder your preference, as most young kittens don't show their real color until around five months of age. Breeders can have a good idea of the future look of their kittens.*
>
> MARIE-LISA LAROCQUE
> *MarieBengal*

Once you've found the Bengal breeder you'd like to work with, you'll need to discuss your ideal cat or kitten. Ideally, you will be able to visit the breeder's home to meet the kittens, but this may not be possible if you do not live nearby. Although Bengals often share a similar set of personality traits, each cat is an individual and will have its own unique personality and quirks. Consider whether you would prefer the most energetic kitten in the litter, the most laidback, or somewhere in between. Do you have a preference of gender? Try not to get too wrapped up in coat color or appearance, as the cat's personality and temperament are most important. It's okay to have a preference, but you may need to be a bit flexible if you want to find the perfect Bengal for your lifestyle.

The breeder will be your most important resource in finding your ideal Bengal. No one knows those specific cats better, so he or she will be in the best position to match you to the companion of your dreams. If you've already discussed your goals and lifestyle with the breeder, he or she may already have a kitten in mind. Relying on the breeder's knowledge and expertise is especially important if you are unable to meet the kittens before purchasing.

Adopting Multiple Cats

In many cases, adopting multiple Bengals can be a great idea. If you have the space and the budget for more than one kitten, you may find that bringing home multiple kittens is the best choice. Cats, especially Bengals, are social animals that enjoy spending time with humans, but most also enjoy the companionship of their own species. Many breeders and rescue organizations actually recommend adopting cats in pairs, especially if you do not have other pets at home already.

When you bring your kitten home, it's important to remember that this is the first time he has been away from his mother and littermates. Moving into a new home can be incredibly stressful, but that stress can be eased somewhat with the presence of a sibling. With multiple kittens, you also won't need to worry about constantly needing to entertain your Bengal. Having a feline playmate will allow you to go to work and do your household chores without worrying about your kitten getting bored.

> 66
>
> *Once you own a Bengal, you have a friend for life; you become their whole world. They are loyal, loving, affectionate, compassionate, and verbal, so they will let you know what they need and when they need it! If you have the kind of lifestyle where you work eight hours during the day, your Bengal will most likely relax and nap most of the day waiting for your arrival. A lot of people with a nine-to-five schedule obtain two Bengals so that they have company until their owner gets home.*
>
> TIFFANI THIEL
> *Baby Bengals OC*
> 99

If you have other cats at home, it may not be necessary to adopt multiple Bengals. However, if your current cats are much older, it may be stressful for them to put up with a rambunctious kitten. Another kitten could help take the pressure off the older cats. Although they will try to engage the older cats in play, they will likely resort to playing with each other when they are denied.

If you are considering adopting multiple Bengals, it's important to be aware that it will also increase your responsibilities. You must then feed and clean up after two kittens. You'll also have to purchase twice the litter and food while also doubling any routine veterinary costs. You will also need to spend time with each kitten on their own so that you can bond with and socialize them properly. Multiple kittens can be an ideal scenario, but you should consider it carefully before committing.

> *Like any cats, Bengals do need plenty of mental stimulation and playtime. Toys and cat towers are great, but in my opinion, having a second cat, preferably of the same age, can't be beat! As a breeder, seeing the interaction between siblings is invaluable! If allowed to grow up together, they can form a great, lasting bond! They will keep each other nicely entertained! I have personally raised two sibling sets of kittens to adults and another pair of kittens one month apart. Their bonds are very tight!*
>
> RHEA SCHMITT
> *Bella Luna Gatte*

CHAPTER 5

Preparing for Your Bengal Cat

Necessary Supplies

> *Many people buy things for regular house cats and are disappointed when they don't use their new 'stuff' ... Bengals are the opposite. They love cat towers, shelves to climb, and toys they can fetch. They love to play and love to be at the highest point in the room when relaxing. They also love to lie in the sun, so window perches are great!*
>
> REBECCA MILLER
> *Jungle Cat Bengals*

O nce you've signed the breeder or adoption contract, you can begin gathering the supplies you'll need for the arrival of your Bengal. It's important to prepare everything ahead of time so that when your kitten arrives, you can focus on getting him settled in rather than rushing to the pet store. If you have other cats already, you probably have most of what you need. However, since it's recommended to separate new cats for at least a few days, you'll need to make sure you have an extra set of supplies available. If this is your first cat, it may be helpful to write out a shopping list to make sure you have everything you need.

One of the most important items on your list will be a pet carrier. It's not recommended to carry a cat in your arms on the way home or to the

*Photo Courtesy of
Sabrina Lawson*

vet, especially if you do not know the cat well. A soft- or hard-sided pet carrier is ideal for safely transporting your Bengal from the breeder or rescue to your house, as well as to any future trips to the vet. Most cats find the enclosed space of a carrier to be calming, as well as keeping you and your cat injury free during travel.

You will also need to make sure you have food for your kitten when he arrives. If you have other cats, you may have a preferred brand already, but you may need to feed your Bengal another type for a short period of time. It's recommended to transition your new cat to his new food over a period of several days to prevent digestive upset, so you will need to ask the breeder or shelter staff what your new cat is currently eating. Additionally, if your other cats' current food is not suited for all life stages, you may need to buy a food formulated specifically for kittens until the Bengal is old enough to eat adult cat food. If you don't already have bowls for food and water, you'll need to purchase a new set. It's worth noting that some cats prefer flat food dishes to prevent whisker fatigue, while others will eat out of a normal bowl without issue. Additionally, some cats struggle to stay hydrated when offered water in a bowl, but a fountain can help increase water consumption.

HELPFUL TIP
Puzzle Toys

Preparing your home for a Bengal cat involves considering their high intelligence and playful nature. Puzzle toys are an excellent way to engage their minds and prevent boredom. Bengal cats thrive with adequate mental stimulation, so by introducing puzzle toys, you can keep your cat mentally engaged and entertained. These toys can also reduce the risk of destructive behaviors and general mischief due to boredom.

If you don't have an extra litter box lying around, you'll need to put that on your shopping list, along with litter. Litter will be discussed in more detail in a later chapter. During the initial period of separation, you'll need to make sure you have an extra litter box for your Bengal. After you have introduced him to your other cats, you can encourage him to use your existing boxes. However, it's still recommended to have more litter boxes than you have cats, so you may need to buy an extra box anyway. Additionally, a stain and odor remover can take care of any clean-up during your Bengal's first few weeks when accidents are most likely to occur.

It's important to provide your Bengal with somewhere comfortable to sleep, so make sure you have a cozy bed ready for him. Most pet stores and online retailers have a variety of styles, and most cats prefer one type over others, but you'll just have to take a guess until you know your new cat better. A covered bed is recommended for nervous or shy kittens, as it provides them with more security and comfort.

Scratching is a natural behavior for cats, so you will want to make sure you have a scratching post for your Bengal. Providing plenty of appropriate scratching areas will help reduce damage to your furniture. Again, cats have their own unique preferences with scratching surfaces, so you'll need to get to know your Bengal better before you know what he likes. Some prefer cardboard, while others prefer sisal rope or carpet. If you have furniture that you would like to protect, many pet retailers sell furniture protectors to prevent scratching.

You should also make sure you have plenty of toys to keep your Bengal busy, especially when you are away or otherwise occupied. Again, most cats have a preference, but catnip toys are generally loved by most cats. You may also want to have a brush or grooming glove to help reduce shedding and get your Bengal used to the grooming process. Treats are also recommended to help with training, socializing, and bonding.

Many cat owners also recommend calming pheromone spray or diffusers. Pheromones can help minimize the stress involved with introducing a new cat into the household. Sprays must be reapplied regularly, while diffusers are plugged into an outlet and generally work for several weeks. These products won't guarantee that introductions will go smoothly, but they can help to reduce stress and tension.

A collar and ID tag are not necessary items but are recommended if you intend to give your Bengal access to the outdoors. Some owners may also prefer for their cats to wear identification in the house in case they accidentally escape. Breakaway collars are recommended for safety. Identification tags should have your contact information so that you can be reached if your lost Bengal is found. If you would prefer for your Bengal to spend only supervised time outdoors, consider purchasing a harness and leash. Most cats can be taught to walk on a leash so that they can explore safely. For cats that spend a significant amount of time outside, flea and tick prevention is also recommended.

Other optional supplies include elevated surfaces such as cat trees or shelves. Bengals are an active breed, and many love to spend their time climbing up to high places in the home. If you don't provide your Bengal with cat-friendly options, you may find that your cat will jump onto counters, tables, and shelves. If you have expensive or sentimental items that you don't want broken, you may want to invest in museum putty to help hold everything in place and prevent your cat from knocking it down.

Finally, you should be prepared to care for your Bengal's dental health at home with dental treats or a toothbrush and toothpaste. Most cats adapt well to the toothbrushing process, but it will take some time to teach your Bengal what to expect and how to behave. If you do not want to spend the time brushing your cat's teeth, consider giving your cat dental treats on occasion. Dental treats are typically chewy or crunchy to help scrape off harmful plaque and tartar. Many also have breath-freshening ingredients.

Here are the recommended supplies for your new Bengal cat:

Necessary Supplies

- Pet carrier
- Food
- Food and water bowls
- Litter box
- Litter
- Bed
- Scratching post
- Toys
- Brush
- Treats

Optional Supplies

- Water fountain
- Calming pheromone spray
- Museum putty
- Collar and ID tag
- Harness
- Cat tree or shelves
- Furniture protectors
- Flea and tick control
- Stain and odor remover
- Dental care products

Preparing Your Other Pets

> " Everything will depend on how the kitten reacts to new things. Never push your cat to take on more than it is willing to endure. We recommend scent swapping when other animals are in the home. It's as simple as giving the kitten's blanket/toy/cat scratcher to the other pet and the other pet's blanket/toy/cat scratcher to the kitten so it can get used to its new friend's smells for a few days. Once your kitten is comfortable, allow it to explore the rest of the home and put your other pet in the safe room so it can further investigate the smells of the new friend. Start with small face-to-face interactions and watch their behaviors. Hissing and growling between cats is normal. You just don't want all-out fighting. For dogs, there shouldn't be any rough play, and providing your Bengal with high places like cat shelves or cat trees where the cat feels safe until it is more comfortable is beneficial.
>
> TABITHA GITTHENS
> *Posh Bengal Spots* "

As mentioned earlier in the chapter, it is recommended to separate your new Bengal from your other pets for at least a few days, if not weeks. Introducing a new cat into the home can be stressful for both the existing pets and the new arrival, and a temporary separation can help the transition go more smoothly. The amount of time that your pets spend separated will depend on how well they get along. For some pets, this may be just a few days, while others may need a week or more before they can safely interact face-to-face. A fearful or aggressive first meeting can create ongoing tension between animals, so it's best to go as slowly as necessary to respect each animal's boundaries.

During the first few hours or days, a solid barrier is recommended. This can be as simple as keeping your new cat in a guest bedroom or bathroom with the door shut. Your existing pets will be able to smell

Photo Courtesy of Julie Filion

the new arrival, but they won't be able to interact. If everyone seems to get along, you can replace the closed door with a baby gate. However, be aware that many cats, and even dogs, can hop over a baby gate with ease. You may need to use two pressure-mounted gates to block the doorway and prevent the animals from going over or under. See-through barriers such as pressure-mounted gates will allow your pets to have some interaction, but they won't be able to seriously injure one another should they respond with fear or aggression. Even with a barrier, you should monitor these early introductions so that you can intervene if something goes wrong. Placing a pheromone diffuser or using a calming spray near the barriers can help ease tension as well. Additionally, you can try offering special high-value treats near the barrier to encourage your pets to spend time near each other for a tasty reward.

Although the animals can see and smell each other through the gates, you can further introduce them by swapping bedding. This will allow your pets to really experience each other's scents without the stress of close contact. Another option is to swap places entirely. Have your existing pets spend time in your Bengal's room while your Bengal explores the rest of the house.

When introducing your new Bengal to your existing cats, it's important to go as slow as necessary to avoid conflict. Once the cats seem to be co-existing without any hissing, growling, or spitting, you can try removing the barrier entirely. It's still possible that they may react aggressively, so supervision is necessary. Do not force the cats into each other's space, as this can result in a fight. If they choose to ignore each other once the barrier is removed, let them. They will interact in their own time, and there is no need to rush them. During the first few days together, you will need to watch them closely for signs of bullying or conflict.

When introducing a new cat to dogs, it's important to exercise caution. Even cat-savvy dogs may have the urge to chase if the cat runs away. If the dog catches the cat, even if in play, serious or fatal injuries can occur. During the first few introductions, it's crucial to keep the dog on a leash. You should also provide the cat with plenty of elevated surfaces to retreat to if the dog shows more interest than the cat would like. Even cats who have lived with dogs for years enjoy having their own space away from their canine family members.

Preparing Your Children and Family

> "
>
> *Bengals are like the Dennis the Menace of cats. They don't tear things up to be mean or malicious; they're just curious and get bored. I recommend baby-proofing the house just like you would for a toddler. Provide lots of environmental enrichment with cat trees, shelves, toys, or even a cat wheel, as these will provide the cat with ways of relieving boredom and getting exercise. When playing with your Bengal, don't allow people to use their hands as toys. This can get your Bengal into the habit of biting and scratching hands and playing too rough.*
>
> ELIZABETH NOLTE
> *Southern Pines Bengals*
>
> "

Although many parents find it tempting to surprise their children with a new kitten, the overwhelming emotions of the moment can frighten a cat. Instead of surprising your kids, it's best to prepare them for the new arrival ahead of time. A nervous or overwhelmed kitten may lash out and scratch or bite, which is not an ideal way to start introductions. The children may still be excited on the day of arrival, but if you've already discussed how to behave and handle the new Bengal, things should go much more smoothly. The conversation you have before picking up your new cat will depend on the age of your children, but it should involve the topic of safety for the sake of the kids as well as the cat.

You will need to explain to your children that they should allow the new cat to approach them first. Calm behavior is necessary so they don't scare the kitten. It's also recommended to discourage your children from picking the kitten up. With particularly young children, you will need to supervise closely and intervene if necessary. You may even have to attempt an introduction at a later time when the child is calmer. Most older children and teenagers are capable of handling the new cat as instructed.

When discussing safe interactions with your children, explain to them that they should speak softly and move a bit slower than normal, especially if the kitten is nervous or shy. You should also discuss that some areas of the cat's body, such as the head and back, are okay to touch, while other parts, such as the tail and belly, may not be. You may want to have your child offer the cat a few treats to encourage interaction—but don't push it if your Bengal seems nervous. Once the cat seems more comfortable, you can also encourage your kids to play with a wand toy or string.

As with dogs, it's recommended to provide your Bengal with areas where it can get away from the kids if necessary. Most cats learn to get along well with children, but they often appreciate a safe space out of reach if they begin to feel overwhelmed. Until you know for certain that your children and your cat are getting along well, supervision is recommended.

Kitten-Proofing Your Home

> "
> *Security should be very important in preparing for a Bengal. Check your windows. These cats can easily tear through normal window screens. Watch going in and out of doors. Never let your cat roam outside freely without your supervision. Be sure to microchip your cat! That will be your best chance of getting it back should it escape or get lost.*
>
> CJ EPPERSON
> *Kharistan Exotics*
> "

Bengal kittens are known for their curiosity and high energy levels, which can get them into trouble on occasion. Before you bring your new cat home, you should go through your house to check for any potential dangers. If you have other pets in your home already, you likely

46

won't have to change much, but you should still go through each room to be certain.

The first step in kitten-proofing your home will be to pick up all small objects that your kitten may try to play with. Children's toys, board game pieces, crayons, and plastic bags are all potential hazards. Your older pets may not feel tempted to chew on plastic bags, but a curious kitten might. Ingesting such an item could result in an intestinal blockage, which could be an expensive vet bill at best and potentially fatal at worst. You don't need to get rid of these small items, but you should at least place them in a container with a lid.

You should also make sure that any houseplants you may have are nontoxic to cats. Toxic plants can cause issues ranging from slight digestive upset to seizures and death, depending on the level of toxicity. Common houseplants that are toxic to cats include croton, ficus, monstera, philodendron, and poinsettia. For a complete list of common toxic houseplants, see the list published on the ASPCA's website.

Photo Courtesy of Bella Sera

Photo Courtesy of
Annette Campaba

A more difficult and ongoing task will be to keep your Bengal kitten out of any potentially dangerous spaces. This can include trash cans, cupboards, laundry bins, and even your washer and dryer. Many kitten owners recommend installing childproof safety locks on any cabinets containing cleaning supplies or medication. If you have windows with mesh screens, you should also double-check the security of the screens. A rambunctious Bengal kitten could easily lean on or run into a loose window screen hard enough to pop it out of place, which could result in a fall or escape. You will also need to continuously make sure that doors to the outside are shut. Garages often contain a number of hazards, including antifreeze and lawn care items, so be sure to keep your kitten out.

While some items are best removed for good, some can be temporarily removed until your kitten understands the rules of the house. You may want to hang curtains higher than normal or remove them completely to prevent your Bengal from destroying them. If you have expensive or sentimental items on shelves, consider moving them or using museum putty to hold them in place. Museum putty is generally inexpensive and will not damage an item. It also will not hold if the cat is determined to push an object off, but it will protect the object from accidental falls.

The First Few Weeks

> *When introducing a Bengal to other pets and people, we highly recommend they stay in a small room/bathroom for the first 48 to 72 hours. During this time, new owners should quietly visit and play with their new companion. Once the kitten/cat feels comfortable, relaxed, and is eating and using the litter box normally, the next phase should begin. In the second phase, we recommend scent swapping, such as rubbing a washcloth on the other pet and allowing the Bengal to smell it in the safe area alone and vice versa. Afterward, we recommend allowing the new Bengal to explore the home on its own with all bedroom doors closed. Once the kitten/cat feels comfortable and relaxed, short visits with the other pet and or people can begin. It is strongly encouraged that the environment be as calm as possible, as first impressions can be difficult to forget. In most cases, Bengal kittens and adults adapt fairly quickly as they often enjoy activity and movement within the home.*
>
> JESSICA PETRAS
> *Liberty Bengals*

The first few weeks with your new Bengal will be the most stressful. As you are getting to know each other, now is the best time to begin establishing your daily routines. If you have other pets in the home, you can also work on introductions. It's also the best time to begin socializing your Bengal to new sights, sounds, and experiences. Depending on the age of your Bengal, you may want to make an appointment with your veterinarian to make sure the cat is up to date on all necessary vaccines.

It's completely normal for a cat of any age to be more withdrawn, shy, or nervous during the first few weeks in a new home. This decompression period is temporary, and once your Bengal gets comfortable, his true personality will appear. Some cats need more alone time during this period, while others may appreciate more affection. You may notice your Bengal hiding behind the sofa or waiting until everyone goes to bed to eat or use the litter box. This is completely normal, and you should not worry unless he does not appear to be eating or using the litter box at all. Do your best to read your cat and meet his needs to the best of your ability.

After a few weeks, you should begin to notice your Bengal settling in. He may be more confident in his behavior and more comfortable seeking attention. It's important to be aware that kittens typically sleep around 20 hours per day, so be sure to give your new companion plenty of time to rest. It can be tempting to interact with a new kitten frequently, especially a high-energy Bengal, but rest is important. During the first few weeks or months with your Bengal, it's recommended to allow him to dictate his desired level of interaction.

CHAPTER 6

Caring for Your Bengal Cat

> *Getting a new Bengal kitten is so exciting. But it is stressful for the kitten. The kitten's entire world is being turned upside down. It's important to keep this in mind when you bring home a new kitten. It will take one to two weeks for a kitten to adjust to a new environment. It is normal for the kitten to meow a lot the first couple of days. Some kittens go on a hunger strike, and they don't want to eat or drink much the first couple of days. Stress can also cause the kitten to have diarrhea. It's best to keep the kitten confined to one room for the first couple of days. Kittens can get overwhelmed if you give them the run of the house. It is very important that you keep the food and litter the same as what the breeder was using for the first two weeks. This is what the kitten is used to, and it will help make the transition easier.*
>
> ERIN H.
> *Sarasota Bengals*

Indoor or Outdoor

One of the most important decisions you will make with your Bengal is whether you will keep him indoors only or allow him time outside. Providing a cat with access to the outdoors can provide plenty of physical and mental exercise, but there are many dangers your Bengal will face.

A typical problem for indoor cats is that they tend to be less active. This means that their owners need to spend time each day meeting their mental and physical needs. Medical conditions such as obesity, heart disease, and arthritis are more common, as are behavioral issues such as marking and scratching.

Photo Courtesy of Jeannie Alexander

HELPFUL TIP
Exceptional
Athleticism

Bengal cats are known for their exceptional athleticism. They are agile jumpers, climbers, and runners and require plenty of physical and mental stimulation to thrive. Providing plenty of vertical spaces, such as cat trees or shelves and interactive toys, will keep them entertained and active.

Although outdoor cats tend to experience fewer weight- and boredom-related issues, they often do not live as long. The reason for this is the sheer number of dangers they are exposed to on a daily basis. The risk of injury due to wildlife, cars, cats, and even stray dogs is incredibly high. Additionally, they are at a higher risk of being exposed to dangerous parasites and viruses such as FIV and rabies. Outdoor cats are also more likely to come into contact with poisonous substances such as rat poison or antifreeze. An attractive and friendly cat such as a Bengal could also potentially be picked up by strangers, who may believe the cat to be a stray.

Outdoor cats are also a serious danger to local wildlife. The American Bird Conservancy has stated that domestic cats are the number one threat to wild birds in North America. It's estimated that domestic cats kill over two billion birds in the United States each year. Unfortunately, cats are considered an invasive predator in many areas and can have serious effects on the populations of threatened and endangered species.

Rather than allow your Bengal to risk his life for a bit of entertainment, there are safer ways to give him outdoor access without complete freedom. If you would rather keep your cat indoors, you can set up areas near a favorite window to bring the outdoors closer. A bird or squirrel feeder outside and a comfortable bed inside will keep your cat busy for hours. However, it won't provide much physical exercise. A more immersive option is to build a "catio" or outdoor enclosure. A catio can be a standalone in a scenic area of your yard, or it can be added to your home and accessed through a pet door or window. Plenty of elevated surfaces in the catio will allow your Bengal to entertain himself with the sights and scents of the outdoors but without the danger. The enclosed space will also prevent wildlife or neighborhood strays from sneaking in the pet door. If your home does not have an outdoor space, you may also

consider training your Bengal to walk on a harness and leash. Some owners even enjoy short hikes with their leash-trained cats.

Despite the dangers, if you choose to allow your Bengal outside, it's
crucial to keep identification on him at all times. A collar and ID tag are a
great choice, but collars can easily get lost. Microchipping is a great way
to make sure you can be contacted if your Bengal gets lost or picked up
by caring strangers. Additionally, you should make sure your outdoor cat
is up to date on all vaccinations as well as flea and tick protection.

Finally, you will need to look over the contract you signed with your
Bengal's breeder. Many breeders require that their kittens be kept indoors
for their own safety. If you do allow your Bengal outside, your breeder may
be able to take legal action against you for violating the terms of the contract.

Emotional and Physical Needs

> *Bengals need mental stimulation. Having as many areas of stim-
> ulation or interest as possible will make for a happy Bengal. Here
> are a few of the happy places I have found my cats love! A win-
> dow where small animals like squirrels can be viewed. A window
> seat or perch with a birdfeeder. A window with bugs flying around
> at night. Amazon boxes and bubbles for popping for a couple of
> days. A wheel that has a good circumference so as not to injure the
> cat's back which has protection for tails and feet from the wheels,
> and that won't derail. I prefer ZiggyDoo due to its guarantee on all
> of the above factors, but there may be other wheels that include all
> of these factors. If limited in space and windows, a daily walk on a
> harness will be something your Bengal will love! You can pick up
> the harness and ask the cat if it wants to go on a walk and it will
> come running. Of course, walks are not always in a straight line.*
>
> PENNY T. LILLY
> *Silverlilly's Bengals*

> "
>
> *Bengals love action, so give them large cat trees to run up and a cat wheel if you have room. Use wand toys to get them jumping and burning energy. If you are able, an outside catio is great fun for them to get out and enjoy watching the birds and getting some sun in a safe space.*
>
> SHERYL KOONTZ
> *Marechal Cattery*

As an active breed, Bengals are often capable of meeting their own physical needs. As long as you can provide him with a high-quality diet, he will often entertain and exercise himself by running and jumping around the house. However, there are plenty of ways you can meet your Bengal's emotional and physical needs without having him bounce off the walls.

It's important to note that each cat will have unique needs. Some cats may need more attention each day, while others are happy to entertain themselves. Not all cats will enjoy the same amount or type of exercise each day either. If you have multiple cats, you may need to provide several options to make sure each cat is happy. As stated in the last chapter, you may also notice a difference in your Bengal's attention-seeking behavior after he settles into his new home. Many cats are standoffish or shy during the first few weeks but soon become confident enough to ask their new owners for more affection. This may require you to adjust the ways in which you meet your cats' emotional and physical needs, so it's important to be flexible. Eventually, you will be able to settle into a regular routine.

In addition to daily play and cuddle time, it can be helpful to provide your Bengal with ways to exercise without getting into trouble. One of the best ways to keep your cat fit and entertained is with a cat exercise wheel. These unique products are similar in appearance to wheels used by pet rodents but much larger. Though they can sometimes be expensive, many cats enjoy running on them. Most cats need a bit of training and positive reinforcement at first, but before long, the cat will be able to run on his own. The wheels are safe for cats to use without supervision, so your Bengal will be able to exercise even when you are away from the house. The wheel also goes only as fast as the cat wants, so each cat can use it at their preferred speed.

Photo Courtesy of Carmen Whitley

A Safe Retreat

> *While Bengals are outgoing and curious in general, it's important to know that they are still cats. They may be shy or want to hide. They may not want to eat or use the litter box. Make sure you place them in a safe, smaller room with everything centrally located, don't overwhelm them, and, like any other new kitten, give them time to acclimate.*
>
> RENEE RORAGEN
> *The Rhine Bengals*

Although Bengals are generally social cats, it's important to provide your new companion with a safe place to retreat to if he wants time to rest and recharge his social battery. This is especially true if you have a busy household with children or other pets. Some cats need just a few hours alone to rest, while others may spend much of their day by themselves.

The safe space you set up for your Bengal will depend on the members of your household and the space you have available. In general, an elevated area such as a cat tree or shelf will deter other pets and children from bothering your Bengal while he rests. Your Bengal may enjoy resting near a sunny window, or he may prefer the enclosed comfort of a covered bed. As you get to know your new companion, you'll be able to determine what he might prefer.

While in his safe retreat, it's important to leave your Bengal alone. You may need to explain to your children that they shouldn't bother the cat if he's in a certain space, but you'll need to enforce this rule with all adults in the home as well. If you have pesky dogs, for example, you may also want to consider installing a pressure-mounted or standalone baby gate. Many gates are available with smaller doors that will keep out larger pets but still allow cats through. These gates can be particularly helpful if you have a dog that likes to get into the litter box. If you have the space available, you may want to consider setting up a safe area large enough for your cat's food, litter box, and bed. That way, he can rest, eat, and relieve himself in peace.

If your Bengal chooses to spend some time alone, it's important not to be offended. As a social breed, most Bengals enjoy spending time with their families, but it's important that they have time to themselves as well. Cats that are constantly overwhelmed with attention can develop behavioral problems due to stress, so it's important to provide a safe retreat.

Photo Courtesy of Annette Campaba

Photo Courtesy of Tammy Smith

Hairballs

As a cat grooms itself, it will inevitably remove loose hair and swallow some of it. Hairballs are an accumulation of hair built up in the digestive system over time. Some of that hair will pass through the digestive system, but sometimes a cat will vomit the hairball up. Although hairballs can be alarming, they are not generally harmful. In fact, it's better for a cat to vomit the hair, as large hairballs could potentially cause an intestinal blockage if they try passing through the digestive system.

Since Bengals are a short-coated breed, they don't usually get hairballs as frequently as long-coated breeds. You may see your Bengal cough up a hairball once a month or even less frequently. If your Bengal begins bringing up hairballs more often, you may want to discuss the matter with your veterinarian. Frequent hairballs can be a sign of gastrointestinal problems but are also often caused by overgrooming, which is a symptom of stress.

When your Bengal coughs up a hairball, you may notice him appearing to gag or choke. He may also stretch his neck out as he attempts to dislodge the hairball. It's important not to be alarmed by this behavior. Hairballs are completely normal, and your cat will not require your help. However, if your cat continually struggles to pass hairballs or loses his appetite or energy, you may need to seek veterinary care.

While shopping for supplies at your local pet store or favorite online retailer, you may notice a number of hairball products. These supplements are designed to help the hairballs dislodge more easily, but most cats can handle hairballs without issue. Unless your vet recommends it, these products are generally unneeded. If you do choose to use a hairball supplement, it's important to follow the instructions on the label, as misuse can cause digestive issues. There are also a number of cat foods on the market formulated with a higher fiber content to help hairballs pass more efficiently through the digestive system.

Enrichment and Playtime

> "
>
> *Bengals enjoy exploring, especially high spaces. Vertical use of space is optimal for them. A sturdy cat wheel is also beneficial to allow them to expend excess energy at will. Bengals also love to have a lot of toys to help keep them entertained. They love playing with their owners, which will strengthen the bond between you and your Bengal.*
>
> KAREN HOAK
> *Keystone Bengals*
> "

> Bengals require a lot of stimulation to keep themselves out of trouble. They can achieve this with a quality cat wheel. We recommend the ZiggyDoo Ferris Cat Wheel or other interactive cat toys.
>
> TABITHA GITTHENS
> *Posh Bengal Spots*

As discussed previously, your Bengal's mental and physical well-being are your responsibility, so it's important that you provide him with adequate enrichment and playtime each day. Wild cats typically hunt for up to six hours per day, satisfying their physical and mental needs. Though most domestic cats do not require quite that much time, it's still important to give them safe opportunities to exercise and express their natural instincts. Playtime is also a great opportunity to bond with your Bengal and share quality time together.

Playtime gives your Bengal the chance to express his natural hunting instincts. Chasing a wand toy or string simulates your cat's natural prey drive. However, it's important not to overdo it. Not all cats enjoy the same style of play. Some cats enjoy a fast and aerobatic chase, while others prefer an easier pace. Always allow your Bengal to set the pace. It's also recommended to give your cat the satisfaction of catching his prey. At the end of the play session, you can let your Bengal catch the toy and carry it away. A treat also works well as a reward for a good hunt. Without this satisfying ending, your Bengal might not be interested in playing with you the next time. It's not as fun for some cats to continually hunt without success, so try to give your Bengal the win.

Puzzle toys can also be a great way to keep your Bengal exercised and entertained, especially when you are unable to interact with him. These toys are usually filled with kibble or treats and must be moved around in a certain way to release the food. Most cat owners who use puzzle toys recommend having several on hand so that they can be swapped out on occasion to keep the cat interested. Puzzle toys can also be made with low-budget items found around the house. Bigger boxes filled with crumpled-up paper or fabric work well, as do shallow boxes with holes cut in them. Don't be afraid to get creative to keep your Bengal busy.

It's important to provide your Bengal with plenty of opportunities to entertain himself, even if he doesn't always take advantage. As mentioned earlier in the chapter, cat exercise wheels are a great way to keep your Bengal fit while you're away. Even a simple birdfeeder outside a window

FUN FACT
Vocalizations

Bengal cats have a range of sounds to express themselves. Your Bengal's vocalizations will go beyond meowing and can include chirps, trills, and howls. Each Bengal vocalization may have a distinct meaning. For example, Bengal cats typically chirp when perceived prey is nearby.

can provide your cat with hours of enrichment. However you choose to entertain your Bengal, be sure you are appealing to both his physical and mental needs. The more variety you can incorporate into your daily routine, the happier and healthier your Bengal will be. Remember, a tired cat is much less likely to get into trouble than an understimulated cat.

CHAPTER 7

Training and Socialization

> "
> *Bengals are extremely intelligent. Most learn to play fetch on their own simply with you throwing toys to them and them realizing it's a repeated process if they bring that toy back to you. You can harness-train them for car rides or walks. It's all about patience, not expecting much, and reaping the rewards when they learn a new trick and continue repeating it.*
>
> TABITHA GITTHENS
> *Posh Bengal Spots*
> "

The Importance of Socialization

Socialization is the best way to ensure that your Bengal is the friendly and confident companion that you desire. It's not something that you can do once and forget about but rather an ongoing process that should be revisited throughout your cat's life. Socialization involves exposing and acclimating your Bengal to new sights, sounds, smells, and feelings, especially those common in everyday life among humans. A well-socialized cat will handle new experiences with confidence, while an unsocialized cat will react with extreme fear and avoidance. Though socialization has the most significant effect on kittens, cats of any age can undergo some level of socialization. For example, a feral kitten may

Photo Courtesy of Kelly Koinm

become comfortable living among humans when socialized young, but an older feral cat may retain that fear and uncertainty regardless of socialization attempts.

Without proper socialization, your Bengal may not be the affectionate and friendly companion you want. Generally, well-socialized cats are safer and easier to handle, both at home and in new environments such as the vet or groomer. Unsocialized cats can lash out as a result of their fear, which puts you and the professionals at risk. Ideally, socialization efforts should begin as soon as you bring your Bengal home. Although your new cat will need to decompress over the first few weeks, you can still begin the process of getting him used to life with a human family.

> *Bengal cats have very little fear when it comes to meeting new animals. They will go right up to a dog they do not know, which could end up in disaster. Take it slow and be cautious.*
>
> SHERYL KOONTZ
> *Marechal Cattery*
>
> *It is good to expose your Bengal kitten regularly to new people when they visit and let the kitten get used to busy activity around the household. The more people the cat is exposed to, the more social it will be as an adult. If a Bengal grows up in a relatively quiet household and is not exposed to other people, it will be shyer as an adult when you have visitors.*
>
> TRACY WILSON
> *Wildtrax*

How to Socialize Your Bengal

Before you begin socializing your Bengal, it's important to understand that learning does not take place when your cat is truly afraid. Most cats can work through a bit of discomfort or uncertainty, but true fear can affect a cat negatively. For this reason, you should be careful about not overwhelming your Bengal. Forcing your cat beyond his tolerance for an experience can result in a negative association, and you will need to work twice as hard to recover his trust. Additionally, some cats need more time to adapt than others. There should never be a set timeline or schedule for socialization. If your Bengal is increasingly uncomfortable with a situation, it's best to back off and attempt it another day. There is no reason to rush this process.

During socialization, you'll need to think about the types of experiences your Bengal will have in his new home. If you have kids or frequent guests, it's important to get him used to a range of noise levels and

Photo Courtesy of Sabrina Lawson

movements. Initially, it's best for your Bengal to experience things from a distance. You can comfort him by getting down on his level, using a calm voice, and offering a few treats if he'll take them. As he gets more comfortable, you can begin asking him to get closer. Having friendly strangers offer him delicious treats is a great way to show him that new people should not be feared. If your Bengal seems afraid, you may need to give him space or try another day. Socialization sessions can be mentally draining, so it's best to keep them short. You can always come back to it later in the day if necessary.

As your Bengal gets more comfortable being handled by people, you can begin socializing him to the experiences he'll have at the vet or groomer. Begin by touching him gently all over his body. Some cats are less comfortable being touched on certain areas of their bodies, so go slowly. You can also use a soft brush to get him used to being groomed. If he seems comfortable being touched, you can progress to picking up his paws and extending his nails. This will prepare him for nail trimming as well as veterinary exams. Next, you can handle his ears as if you were examining the inside. If he seems comfortable, you may try to lift his lips and expose his teeth. Throughout this process, be sure to offer plenty of praise and affection.

Some cats are more sensitive to sound than others, but you'll want to begin exposing your Bengal to sounds he may hear often in his new home. Unsocialized cats may react to loud noises such as the vacuum, blender, or music. Again, it's best to approach these sounds from a distance and get closer as your Bengal gets more comfortable. The internet is a great way to expose your cat to a variety of new sounds. There are many videos that can be found on YouTube that are designed specifically for socializing pets. You can play the videos at a low volume and turn them up as your cat gets comfortable.

> **"**
>
> *Always take it slow when you are introducing other animals to your Bengal cat. Try to make it fun with toys and treats. When you are introducing your Bengal cat to a new person, give the cat time to warm up to the person. Do not allow the new person to pick the cat up right away. Have the new person play with the cat first and give the cat a treat. The best way to bond with a Bengal cat is through play.*
>
> ERIN H.
> *Sarasota Bengals*
>
> **"**

Training Your Bengal

> *Bengals are very smart and can pick up on things very quickly. They are very dog-like and can be trained almost like a dog can, such as playing fetch, walking on a leash, doing tricks, and so on. If your Bengal thinks the new activity is fun, it will learn to do it quickly.*
>
> KAREN HOAK
> *Keystone Bengals*

Although many people do not think of cats as trainable, it's actually possible to teach your Bengal a wide range of commands. Cats will not participate in training sessions if they are not enjoying them, so you must be sure to keep your sessions as fun and engaging as possible. This means you should avoid training at times of the day when your cat is tired or distracted. You may also want to stay away from mealtimes so that your cat is more likely to work for a treat. Additionally, it can be helpful to use a specific high-value treat only for training sessions. Using your Bengal's favorite food will help to encourage him to take part in training. Some owners choose to use cooked chicken breast or canned tuna, while others use their cat's favorite dry treat. It may take some time to figure out what motivates your Bengal, but once you know, you can use it to your advantage.

It's also recommended to keep training sessions as short as possible. Most cats do not enjoy repetition, so it's best to train for only as long as your cat can remain focused and interested in the work. Kittens have a particularly short attention span, so you may be limited to one to two minutes per session. This may not seem like much, but you can always revisit what you're working on later in the day. You should also make sure to end every session on a good note. If your cat doesn't seem to be understanding what you want him to do, try asking for something he knows well. Once he performs the task, you can reward him and end the session. You may need to reconsider the session and how you can modify your training next time so that your Bengal better understands your request. Additionally, you always want to end the session before your cat loses interest so that he will be more likely to participate later.

When you first begin training your Bengal, it's recommended to work in low-distraction environments. That way, you will not be competing with things that your cat may find more interesting. As your cat starts to understand what you're asking of him, you can begin introducing more distractions. For example, if your end goal is to show off your cat's tricks to your friends, you can start by asking your Bengal to perform in front of a single person he knows well rather than going straight to performing for an audience.

It's also recommended to focus on one skill at a time. If you were to try to teach your Bengal several commands at once, he could become confused and frustrated. However, if you work on one until he has a good understanding, then he will be able to learn the next command more easily. Remember, you want to set your cat up for success. It's important you understand that your Bengal will learn at his own pace and in his own way. If you have multiple cats, you may need to try different training methods with each of them until you figure out what works best. Some cats can pick up a new command in a single session, while others may take a few days to grasp it.

Clicker Training Basics

Clicker training is one of the most popular training methods due to its high rate of success. It's not only used to train cats and dogs but also exotic animals such as dolphins and elephants. Once an animal has been taught the value of the clicker, the noise itself positively reinforces a behavior by marking the exact moment in time when the correct behavior was performed. The greatest benefit of using a clicker is that you can use it to tell your Bengal he's done well, even if it takes you a moment to pull a treat out of your pocket. Without that marker, you risk your cat misunderstanding the interaction.

*Photo Courtesy of
Lisa Ferrigno*

The clicker is not inherently valuable to an animal, so you'll need to spend time "loading" the clicker before you actually begin using it to train. If you do not increase the value of the clicker first, it's nothing more than an obnoxious noise to your cat. The time it takes to bring value to the clicker will depend on your cat. Some cats understand it in just a few days, while others need more time. Thankfully, it's something you can work on in short sessions throughout the day.

The first time you introduce your Bengal to the clicker, you want to make sure he's paying attention to you. The rustle of a treat bag should be enough to draw his focus. Prepare yourself with a treat in one hand and the clicker in the other. Press the clicker and immediately reward your cat with the treat. The first several sessions will be relatively simple as you introduce your Bengal to the idea that the clicking noise means he gets a treat. Once he understands that, you can begin to introduce commands.

Luring is one of the best ways to teach your cat a new behavior. This training concept consists of luring your cat into position with a treat. If you'd like to teach your cat to sit on command, for example, you can lure him into position by holding a treat above his head. You'll want it to be low enough that he won't stand on his hind legs but high enough that he'll need to look up to see it. Some cats may try to grab your hand with their paws, but with a little practice, you should be able to figure out the correct hand position to get your cat to sit. Once his back end touches the ground, press the clicker and immediately reward him.

Targeting is another training concept commonly used alongside clicker training. The only additional tool you'll need is a targeting stick, which can be made or bought. As with the clicker, you'll need to first teach your cat how to interact with the object. Many targeting sticks have a ball at the end to give the animal a visible target. Once your cat understands the value of the clicker, you can present him with the targeting stick. At first, you'll want to reward any interest in the stick. If your cat looks at or sniffs the stick, immediately click and reward. Many cats learn quickly to touch the target with their nose to get a reward. After several sessions working on this, you can use the stick to lure your Bengal into learning other commands, like jumping from one surface to another.

Scratching and Bad Behavior

> **"**
>
> *Training a Bengal has more to do with the trainer than the Bengal. Bengals will become bonded to their owner and aim to please. Showing a Bengal what it can do is much more effective than punishment. A Bengal views punishment as aggression and does not remain bonded if it feels like the human is hostile. Give the Bengal a substitute for what you may not want it to do. If you do not want it on the countertops, put a window seat or perch where it can sit and watch. The cat only wants to be with you. Place the Bengal off the counter onto its special place and tell the cat the place is for it. A couple of times of doing this, and the cat will learn. A perch near the table will suffice for being on the table. Keeping a positive relationship with preventive measures will keep your Bengal wanting to please and build a trusting relationship.*
>
> PENNY T. LILLY
>
> *Silverlilly's Bengals*
>
> **"**

Although many cat owners view scratching as an undesirable behavior, it's completely natural for cats of all breeds. Cats use scratching to remove dead and damaged sections of their claws, as well as to mark objects with their scent. The stretching action also helps to relieve stress, and it simply feels good. Unfortunately, scratching can quickly become a problem in the home when it leads to damaged furniture and flooring. Rather than discouraging your Bengal from scratching entirely, you should provide him with appropriate places to scratch. Scratching posts and cat trees are great options, but you may also need to discourage scratching on furniture by temporarily or permanently covering the sections your cat likes to scratch.

In order to facilitate that stress-relieving stretch, most cats prefer tall objects for scratching. Scratching posts of at least 32 inches in height are usually tall enough for most Bengals. You'll also want to make sure any

*Photo Courtesy of
Bella Sera*

cat furniture is sturdy. Most cats will not enjoy scratching on a wobbly object. Additionally, many cats prefer to scratch certain surfaces over others, so you may need to try a variety of materials at first. Corrugated cardboard, carpet, and sisal rope are popular choices. When introducing your Bengal to a new scratching post, you can encourage him to scratch by rubbing the surface with a bit of catnip or having him chase a toy around and on it. Do not try to force your Bengal to scratch the post, as you may inadvertently upset him and cause him to avoid the post entirely.

If your Bengal's natural scratching behavior has become destructive and you cannot get him to accept appropriate scratching areas, you may want to consult a feline behaviorist. Seeking professional advice is always recommended over declawing. The harmful effects of declawing will be discussed in a later chapter.

In addition to scratching, some Bengals take other natural behaviors, such as vocalization, to the extreme. All cats will meow or cry at times, and some breeds tend to be more vocal than others. However, a sudden increase in vocalization could indicate that something is wrong. Meowing can be a simple sign of boredom, and your Bengal may be demanding attention, but it can also be a sign of pain or discomfort. If your Bengal has suddenly become noisier than normal, you may need to schedule an appointment with your veterinarian or examine whether all your cat's needs are being met.

Urinating or defecating outside the litter box can be considered bad behavior, though it's often a cat's way of saying something is wrong. If you are not cleaning your Bengal's litter box frequently enough, he may begin making messes elsewhere. However, it can also be a sign of stress. During significant changes in your cat's life, such as moving or the addition of a new family member, your Bengal may relieve himself outside of the box. It's important to note that urinating outside of the litter box can also be a sign of urinary problems such as a UTI or bladder stones. If the reason for your Bengal's bad behavior is not clear to you, it's best to have your veterinarian rule out any health problems.

Cats do not generally behave badly simply because they want to. Most bad behaviors are a reaction to stress or changes in the household. If there are no underlying health problems, your Bengal may simply be behaving badly as his way of telling you that he's not happy. In most cases, once the stressor has been removed or the cat has adjusted to the change, the bad behavior resolves itself. However, if you are struggling with your Bengal's behavior and cannot resolve the issue on your own, you may want to seek the advice of a feline behaviorist.

FUN FACT
Truth or Myth: Water

It's widely believed that Bengal cats love water, but is this truth or myth? Generally, Bengal cats enjoy the water more than their other domestic counterparts. While the cause of this affinity is unclear, many believe that Bengal cats enjoy the water because of the exploratory nature of their ancestor, the Asian leopard. However, keep in mind that not all Bengal cats are aquatic aficionados.

CHAPTER 8

All about the Litter Box

Types of Litter Boxes

> 66
>
> *You will want to have a litter box about every 10 feet at first in the areas you initially let the kitten become acclimated to. Kittens have very short memories, and you should place them in the box. Keep any piles of clothes picked up that the kitten might confuse with a place to go potty. Dirty clothes, socks, and underwear might seem like a litter box until the kitten gets to be about six months old. Good habits are important to keep, and bad habits are harder to correct.*
>
> PENNY T. LILLY
> *Silverlilly's Bengals*
>
> 99

There are many different styles of litter box on the market, and not all cats like the same type. It's possible that your new Bengal may not like the type of litter box that you've put in place for him. Many cat owners opt to give their cats choices by setting up at least two different styles of litter boxes in their home, especially if there are multiple cats in the home. The general rule of thumb is to have one more litter box than you have cats. For example, you would have two litter boxes for a single cat and three boxes for a pair of cats.

Size is one of the most important features to consider when shopping for litter boxes. Ideally, the box should be large enough for your Bengal to turn around and dig without having to step in any waste. If the litter box is too small, your cat may decide to relieve himself somewhere else.

You'll also need to consider the height of the litter box's walls. Some cats "spray" when they urinate, which can create a mess if the walls are too low. Cats that kick a lot of litter around may also need higher walls to prevent messes. Top-entry litter boxes are also great for cats with messy bathroom habits. However, you'll also need to consider your Bengal's mobility. Young kittens, obese adults, and senior cats may not be able to climb into top-entry boxes or those with high sides.

Your Bengal may also have a preference for a covered or uncovered litter box. Some cats prefer the privacy of a covered box, while others would prefer to keep an eye on everything around them. If you choose a covered litter box for your Bengal, it's important to make sure the box itself, as well as the opening, are large enough. Depending on the type of litter you use, you should also be aware that covered boxes can worsen any respiratory issues your cat may have. A low-dust litter and frequent cleaning are always recommended for use with covered litter boxes.

CELEBRITY BENGAL

Suki the Adventure Cat

A Bengal cat from Alberta, Canada, has made headlines with her passion for travel. Suki's owner, Martina Gutfreund, documents their journeys with photographs that capture the beauty of various landscapes worldwide, from snowcapped mountains to lush forests. Gutfreund adopted Suku in 2017 and trained her to walk on a leash before embarking on their global adventures.

If you have the budget, you may also want to consider a self-cleaning litter box. These electronic boxes can be expensive, but they ensure that your Bengal will always have a clean box to use. It's also important to note that many self-cleaning litter boxes must only be used with a specific type of litter, which is often expensive as well. However, if you have a cat with any health issues that you need to monitor, a self-cleaning litter box can make it difficult to keep an eye on bathroom habits.

When deciding on a litter box for your new Bengal, you may also need to consider the bad habits of your other pets. If you share your home with dogs, you may need to find a box that will keep your dog out of it. Many dogs have a bad habit of raiding the litter box, so there are plenty of options on the market to keep them out. However, if your dog is determined to find himself a snack, you may need to either elevate the box or use a baby gate to prevent access. As mentioned in an earlier chapter, there are baby gates designed to allow small animals access while preventing larger animals from getting in. You can also try mounting a regular gate several inches off the floor so that your cat can squeeze under but your dog cannot.

Another option to consider is to toilet train your cat and make litter boxes obsolete in your home. However, you will need to temporarily use litter boxes while you toilet train your Bengal. There are special types of litter boxes that fit over a toilet seat, which will help with training. Typically, there are several in a set. The first generally covers the toilet's opening completely, and subsequent boxes have an increasingly large hole in the middle. You will need to use a flushable litter, but as the opening in the box becomes larger, you can use less and less litter. Eventually, your cat will be able to relieve himself on any toilet. Again, it's important to use only litter that is safe for flushing, or else you may have a serious plumbing issue.

Litter Options

> **"**
>
> *I use World's Best Litter for kittens under the age of three months. Very young kittens will eat litter, and World's Best is safer for them because it is a natural corn-based product. As they get older, I switch to Fresh Step Unscented clumping litter.*
>
> ERIN H.
>
> *Sarasota Bengals*
>
> **"**

Once you've chosen a box, you'll need to decide what type of litter you'd like to use. Many cats have a preference, though some will use any type of litter. The most commonly used type of litter is clay. It was the first commercially available cat litter and has been available since 1947. It can be found in any pet store as well as grocery stores, convenience stores, and even farm and ranch stores. Clay litter is generally the least expensive option, and you can choose from clumping and non-clumping options. The downside of clay is that it's very heavy, dusty, and prone to tracking.

Another popular choice is crystal or silica litter. The crystals are made of quartz sand. Crystal litter is highly absorbent and is not as heavy as clay. It's also a low-odor and low-dust option, but it does not clump and is prone to be tracked out of the litter box. Most users recommend daily mixing to make sure the moisture in the box is evaporating correctly. Crystal litter can be somewhat expensive, and some cats do not like how it feels.

Pelleted litter comes in a variety of materials, including paper, pine wood, and tofu. The pellets are nontoxic, low dust, and lightweight. The larger size discourages tracking, but since the pellets do not clump, they can be somewhat difficult to clean. Paper pellets are the cheapest option and are a great option for cats with respiratory issues or those recovering from surgical procedures. Unfortunately, paper does little to control odor. Pine pellets are better for odor due to the natural pine scent. Tofu pellets are a newer option on the market and are made from soybean

fibers. Tofu litter is biodegradable and can be flushed. It does clump when wet as well. The downsides to tofu pellets are typically the price as well as the risk of spoilage if it gets wet in storage.

Walnut and corn litter are other all-natural options. As the names suggest, they are made from crumbled walnut shells and corn cobs. Both options are sustainable, biodegradable, and low dust. Corn litter clumps well, and walnut can be either clumping or non-clumping. As with tofu pellets, both options can be spoiled if they get wet in storage. Additionally, both corn and walnut litter are prone to being tracked out of the box.

While you should consider your own preference, your priority in choosing a litter should always be your Bengal's comfort and safety. Low-dust options are recommended for any cat, but especially those with respiratory issues. Some cats eat their litter, so if your Bengal is guilty of this bad habit, you'll need to look for nontoxic options, such as corn crumbles or pine pellets. Additionally, clumping litters can be danger-ous if swallowed, as they can cause intestinal blockages. Low-tracking litters are also recommended if you aren't a fan of sweeping up the litter box area daily.

Litter Box Training

> **"**
>
> *As soon as you bring your Bengal home, put it into the litter box and allow the cat to explore from there. This will guarantee your Bengal can find the way back to the litter when it is time to use it.*
>
> REBECCA MILLER
> *Jungle Cat Bengals*
> **"**

Most cats are introduced to the litter box at a young age, so it's likely that your Bengal already has some knowledge of how to use it. However, using a litter box is a natural behavior, so it's not difficult to introduce. Cats have a natural instinct to bury waste, so they tend to pick up on the litter box easily.

When introducing your cat to the litter box for the first time, it's important not to force him inside. This will only create a negative association and will discourage him from using the box appropriately. Instead, set him near the box and just quietly observe him. Most Bengals will be curious enough to explore the box on their own. To further encourage your cat to use the litter box, set him near it after a meal or nap when he will likely need to go. Once inside the box, your Bengal's natural instincts will likely take over, but when he's finished, you can reward him with plenty of praise. Be sure to wait until he's done to reward him so you don't accidentally interrupt him.

Accidents are inevitable, but it's important not to get upset with your Bengal. He's still learning and will make mistakes on occasion. Punishment is not acceptable and will only cause emotional damage. You will only create fear rather than teach him what is right. However, it's important to clean the area as well as possible to discourage your Bengal from going there again. Enzymatic cleaners are recommended as they help to break down odor-causing particles and remove stains.

Common Problems

> **❝**
>
> *Commercial diets add a lot of unnecessary fillers that Bengals don't need, and you will find that's why they have really smelly poops. Balanced raw diets eliminate a large amount of smell, and poo is much smaller because the cat's body is actually utilizing the food it is eating and not just turning it into waste.*
>
> TABITHA GITTHENS
> *Posh Bengal Spots*
>
> **❞**

One of the most common reasons that any cat will struggle with litter box training is that it dislikes something about the box. It may not be clean enough, or the cat may simply not like either the litter or the box. Some cats are more sensitive to the odor or the feel of the litter and may not want to use it. For some, the location may also be an issue. Many cats prefer to relieve themselves in a private space, so if the litter box is out in the open, it may be too stressful.

If you believe that cleanliness may be the issue, you may simply need to scoop the box more frequently. If this is not possible, you may also want to consider investing in a self-cleaning litter box. It's generally recommended to scoop out feces and urine at least once per day, but some may require more frequent cleanings. Even with regular scooping, you will also need to replace the litter on occasion to prevent the buildup of odor and bacteria. If it has been some time since you replaced the

litter, you may want to see if that will help encourage your Bengal to use the box.

It's also possible that your Bengal may be suffering from a medical condition that makes it difficult to get to the litter box in time. Messes are not always a sign of bad behavior, so you may want to have your veterinarian examine your cat before addressing the problem as behavioral or environmental. Cats do not always make it obvious when they feel unwell, so a check-up may be the answer.

Toxoplasmosis

Toxoplasmosis is a common parasitic infection. The disease is caused by the parasite *Toxoplasma gondii* and is commonly passed to humans through the consumption of undercooked meat. However, it's also possible to contract the parasite by handling cat feces. Not all people infected with toxoplasmosis will show symptoms, but symptoms most often resemble the flu. Children, seniors, and people with immunodeficiencies are most at risk for serious illness. Additionally, pregnant people may be at risk for serious birth defects and miscarriage. Treatment is relatively simple and typically consists of oral medication.

If your Bengal is kept inside, it's unlikely that he will pick up the parasite. Outdoor cats are at a higher risk due to exposure to wildlife that is already infected. Washing your hands after handling your cat's litter is always recommended, but if you are at risk for infection, you may also want to wear gloves and a face mask. Since pregnant people are most at risk for serious complications, it's recommended to avoid stray cats and resist the temptation to introduce new cats into the household until after the baby is born.

CHAPTER 9

Grooming Your Bengal Cat

Brushing

> "
> The best thing about Bengals is that they tend to groom them-
> selves. Bengals have short hair, and they don't shed very much.
> They are very clean animals. During certain times of the year
> (spring and summer), they shed more. During this time, I recom-
> mend you brush them once a week to remove excess hair.
>
> ERIN H.
> Sarasota Bengals
> "

Regular brushing is an essential aspect of keeping your Bengal cat's skin and coat as healthy as possible. Brushing stimulates blood flow in the skin and distributes natural oils through the coat, as well as removing dirt, dander, and loose hair. Though most cats groom themselves, brushing will help keep shedding under control. It can also help reduce the occurrence of hairballs since the cat will not swallow as much loose hair.

As your Bengal reaches his senior years, regular grooming is even more important, as many older cats have a difficult time grooming them-selves. Without regular grooming, the coat can become tightly matted, which can be painful. Unfortunately, tight matting cannot be brushed out

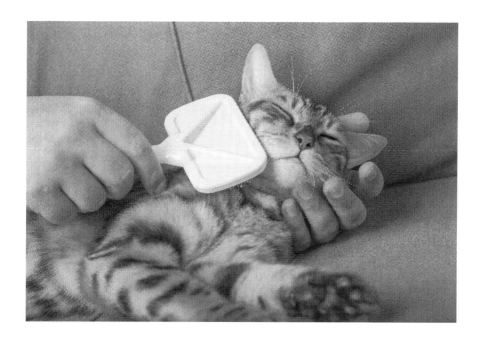

and must be shaved for the comfort of the cat. Most Bengals are able to prevent matting through frequent self-grooming, but you may need to help your cat if he is unable to do so himself.

Most groomers recommend brushing your Bengal at least once or twice per week, but the frequency depends on your cat's overall coat condition. Many cats enjoy being brushed, so you may even brush your Bengal daily if it's a process you both enjoy. If you notice your Bengal developing mats in certain areas, you may need to brush him more frequently. Difficult-to-reach areas such as the hips and spine are commonly matted areas for cats suffering from limited mobility.

In order to keep your Bengal's coat shiny and mat-free, it's important to use the right tools and brushing methods. Many cat owners make the unfortunate mistake of only brushing the top layer of the coat, which can leave painful mats near the skin that must be shaved out. Slicker brushes are highly recommended, as well as metal combs. Both come in a wide variety of sizes and shapes to suit each cat and owner. The best way to ensure a tangle-free coat is to use the slicker brush first and check your work afterward with the metal comb. Be sure that the brush is reaching the skin, but be careful not to press too hard. Both slicker brushes and

HELPFUL TIP
Brushing Your Miniature Leopard

Grooming Bengal cats, sometimes called "miniature leopards" due to their unique patterning, is relatively straightforward. Your Bengal should be brushed twice to thrice weekly with a soft, short-bristled brush to remove dead hair and prevent matting. In addition, some experts recommend brushing your cat both with and against the grain of the hair to stimulate hair regrowth and thoroughly remove all loose hair.

combs can scratch a cat's skin with too much pressure.

Although deshedding tools are found in many pet stores, they aren't typically recommended as they can damage your Bengal's coat. Many deshedding brushes will break the coat rather than remove loose hair. They can also scratch the skin if they are used with too much pressure. If you are unsure of which tool to use, ask your local cat groomer or your Bengal's breeder for their recommendation.

Bathing

> "
>
> *Bengals don't need to be bathed very often. Bathing too often can dry out the skin and coat. An occasional bath if the coat is soiled or is very oily is enough. If the skin is very dry and flaky, see your vet about getting a medicated shampoo. Over-the-counter shampoos can make it worse. Do not use coconut oil. It will make the skin too oily, and it can cause skin irritation. The strong scent can also irritate the respiratory tract. Don't use Dawn dish soap, as it can seriously dry out the skin and coat. Use cat-specific shampoos. Don't blow dry the coat. Blow drying will make the coat very fluffy instead of giving it that nice sleek look. A chamois cloth can be used to sleek down the coat.*
>
> ELIZABETH NOLTE
> *Southern Pines Bengals*
>
> "

*Photo Courtesy of
Katie Childress*

Bengals are clean cats with low-maintenance coats, so they rarely require baths. Many cats go their entire lives without being bathed, but there may be an occasion when your Bengal gets into something that needs to be washed from his coat. If you are showing your Bengal, you may also need to bathe him on occasion to ensure he looks his best in the ring.

Not all shampoos are safe for use on cats, so it's important to use only products labeled for cats. Cats are more sensitive to certain chemicals than dogs, so it's not recommended to use dog shampoo unless it's also labeled for use on cats. It's also recommended to use shampoos with more natural ingredients to reduce the likelihood of skin irritation.

When bathing your Bengal, be sure to wet the coat thoroughly before applying shampoo. The moisture in the coat will help distribute the shampoo more easily. Unless your Bengal is particularly messy, it's best to avoid the head so that you don't accidentally spray water or shampoo into the ears and face. Depending on the shampoo, you may also need to dilute it, otherwise, it can be difficult to rinse. As with brushing, you'll want to make sure the product reaches the skin, so be sure to massage the product into the coat after application. When rinsing, it's recommended to rinse until you believe the shampoo is gone, and then continue rinsing to be sure. Product left in the coat can cause skin irritation and digestive upset if it is ingested during self-grooming.

Conditioner is optional, depending on your cat and the type of shampoo you're using. If your Bengal doesn't enjoy bathing, you may want to opt for a leave-in conditioner that can be sprayed on afterward rather than having to subject him to more time in the bathtub or sink. It's also important to note that some conditioners increase drying time, so if it's chilly out, you may not want to use a rinse-out conditioner.

Many Bengals enjoy spending time in the water, so you may find that your cat behaves well during a bath. However, some can react badly and may lash out, so be careful when bathing your Bengal for the first time. If your Bengal is in need of a bath but is difficult to handle, you may want to consider hiring a professional cat groomer. Finding a good cat groomer will be discussed later in the chapter.

Drying

After the bath, you will need to thoroughly dry your Bengal's coat. Remember, a wet coat can make your cat more sensitive to cold, so try to provide him with warm places to dry as quickly as possible. A sunny window may be enough for some cats, but you may also need to be more thorough with towel drying. Rough handling during towel drying can upset some cats, so be sure to work in smooth and gentle motions. Many cats will work to dry themselves with frantic licking after the bath, so don't be surprised if your Bengal begins self-grooming right away.

A hairdryer can also be a great way to dry your Bengal's coat if he will tolerate it. However, human hairdryers can get too hot, so be sure to keep the dryer far away from your cat's skin. Using one hand on the dryer and one hand on your cat can help you monitor the temperature as well as aid in fluffing the coat.

Trimming or Clipping

It is not recommended to trim or clip your Bengal's coat. Bengals are short-coated cats that do not require haircuts. As stated earlier in the chapter, if your Bengal becomes severely matted, shaving the coat may be the most humane thing to do. However, it's important to be aware that clipping can permanently affect the coat. Many cats can be clipped without a permanent change in growth or texture, but not all. Additionally, cats have very thin skin that can be easily cut by an unskilled groomer.

Photo Courtesy of Jessica Black

If you are having trouble caring for your Bengal's coat, seeking the help of a professional cat groomer is recommended.

Nail Care

> **"**
>
> *We play with our Bengals' feet and faces on a regular basis. This makes it much easier if your Bengal ever has an injury or illness or needs a nail trim. If the cat is used to having positive touch in the face and feet area, it will not be difficult to handle its feet when needed or to administer medication.*
>
> REBECCA MILLER
> *Jungle Cat Bengals*
> **"**

If your Bengal's scratching has become an issue, trimming his nails can help reduce the damage to you and your furniture. If your Bengal is well-behaved, you can trim his nails yourself or you can take him to a groomer or vet. Nail trims are not usually expensive, and many facilities take walk-ins, though you should always call ahead to verify.

If you are interested in trimming your Bengal's nails yourself, you'll need to purchase nail clippers. There are two types: scissor style and guillotine style. Scissor-style nail trimmers are recommended, as guillotine-style clippers can crush the nail if they are not sharp enough. Scissor-style clippers are the overall safer tool, especially for inexperienced users.

Many cats tolerate nail trims, but some may struggle a bit. To prevent scratches, you can wrap your Bengal in a towel or blanket and expose just one paw at a time. If you have a helper, one person can hold the cat, and the other can trim. It's also recommended to work in a quiet area with minimal distraction in order to reduce stress.

To expose the nail, gently hold your Bengal's paw and press on the toe. Take a good look at the nail to see how much you can trim. At the base of the nail, you'll see a pink triangular area. This is the nail's blood supply and is called the quick. If you cut the quick, the nail will bleed, so it's important to cut at least one-eighth of an inch in front of it. Leaving more is fine; you just want to trim away the sharp hook at the end of the nail. Snip the nail quickly, as hesitation can cause your Bengal to pull back. As you trim your cat's nails, don't forget the dewclaws.

Cutting the quick can be painful for your cat, but accidents do happen. Styptic powder or gel will stop the bleeding, so it can be helpful to have these products on hand, just in case. You may also use cornstarch, though it's not quite as effective. A small amount on the tip of the nail should be enough to slow and stop the bleeding. It's best to hold your cat for a few moments after application. If he licks the powder off the nail too soon, bleeding may resume.

If nail trims haven't reduced your Bengal's scratching problem, you may want to consider using nail caps. These pain-free plastic covers can be applied to your cat's nails at home or by your vet or groomer. They stick to the nail with nontoxic adhesive and must be reapplied every four to six weeks. Nail caps do not prevent the nail from being retracted, but they do prevent scratching damage to furniture and people. They are available in a range of colors and sizes to suit all cats and owners. Depending on your Bengal's behavior, you can apply the caps to just the front paws or all four. Though the caps do not cause pain, some cats will be a bit fussy for a few days following the first application. Most cats get used to the feeling quickly.

Most nail caps require the nails to be trimmed before application. To apply the caps, you'll want to place a small amount of adhesive inside each cap before sliding it onto the nail. If the glue seeps from the sides of the cap after it's placed on the nail, you should use less on the next one. It typically only takes a few minutes for the adhesive to dry.

If your Bengal is an outdoor cat, it's not recommended to trim the nails or use nail caps. You would be removing your cat's main defense against predators, which could put him in serious danger. Nail trims and caps should be used only on indoor cats.

Ear and Eye Care

> Bengals don't require a lot of grooming; they tend to keep themselves pretty clean. Watch their ears for any waxy buildup and gently swab out the ears with a Q-tip to wipe away any buildup. Trim the cat's nails as needed every two to three weeks to protect against any furniture scratching.
>
> TABITHA GITTHENS
> *Posh Bengal Spots*

If your Bengal is healthy, there should be no need to clean his eyes or ears. However, you should be monitoring his health daily so that you can address any issues as soon as possible. As you pet your cat each day, casually check both his eyes and ears for anything unusual. With the ears, it's important to check the outer and inner structures for redness, swelling, or discharge.

If you notice any issues with your Bengal's eyes or ears, call your veterinarian as soon as possible. Eye and ear problems can worsen quickly, so the sooner they're treated, the better. Your veterinarian will need to examine your Bengal to determine the diagnosis and treatment. Common issues such as infection or mites cannot be dealt with at home.

However, if your cat's ears or eyes are simply dirty, you can clean them at home. There are many eye and ear products on the market that can be used with cats, but as stated earlier in the chapter, it's important to use only products made for cats. Using a cotton ball dampened with the product of your choice, you can gently wipe away dirt. With the ears, always use a cotton ball rather than a cotton swab. With a cotton ball, you will never be able to reach far enough into the ear to cause damage or injury. After wiping, you can use a dry cotton ball to clear out any excess product.

Finding a Groomer

Not all pet groomers are able or willing to work with cats, so you may need to do some research to find a cat groomer in your area. However, in some areas, you may be able to find groomers that work exclusively with cats. For the safety of your Bengal, it's recommended to only work with groomers familiar with safe cat handling. Grooming a cat is not the same as grooming a dog, and different handling methods are required. The National Cat Groomers Institute is one of the leading organizations in safe cat grooming. Their website has a list of Certified Feline Master Groomers around the world, so if you're looking for a highly skilled groomer, their list is a great place to start.

Some groomers will work in stationary locations, while others may have mobile businesses. If your groomer of choice is mobile, you will be able to have the groomer come to your home. Otherwise, you will need to transport your Bengal to the groomer's location. It's important to note that most mobile groomers charge more, but the price will vary according to your location and the services you have requested.

If your Bengal is difficult to groom, you may want to talk to your veterinarian. Your vet may be able to prescribe a sedative that can be given prior to grooming. Many vet clinics also have groomers in-house, which can be ideal if any issues arise during sedation.

Photo Courtesy of
Joe Mueller

CHAPTER 10

Feeding Your Bengal

Benefits of Quality Nutrition

> "
>
> *The best advice I can give on nutrition is to feed a raw diet. My cats have become so much healthier and have bounced back from having kittens so much faster since I started feeding raw. Raw food is a more natural way of eating for your cat and light-years better for its health than any dry kibble, as long as it has the proper number of vitamins and minerals in it. I also use a vitamin called Nuvet, which I have found to be of very high quality.*
>
> AMY CHASTAIN
> *BestBengals4u*
>
> "

Nutrition has an immense effect on any cat's health and happiness, especially when they are young. The effects of an imbalanced diet are not always visible right away, and some deficiencies can affect your cat's development permanently. Since nutrient imbalances can be particularly harmful to growing kittens, it's important to make sure your Bengal is fed a high-quality, balanced diet starting the moment you bring him home.

To keep your Bengal as healthy as possible, you'll also need to make sure you're feeding him the correct portion sizes. Obesity can have serious effects on your cat's health and well-being but is easily prevented with proper portion control and exercise. Weight management will be discussed later in this chapter, but it's important to remember that even the healthiest food can be harmful if fed incorrectly.

If you are unsure about the quality of your Bengal's food or have questions about certain ingredients, it's recommended to consult a feline nutritionist. Your veterinarian will also have a basic education in nutrition, but if you have more in-depth questions, it's best to talk to a specialist. To find a feline nutritionist near you, visit the website of the American College of Veterinary Nutrition (ACVN), where you can find a list of board-certified veterinary nutritionists.

Photo Courtesy of Jennifer Gray

The Obligate Carnivore

> *We have bred Maine Coons and rescued countless cats over the last 20-plus years. In our experience, Bengals are prone to digestive upset and do best on a high-quality, single-protein diet with limited ingredients and preservatives. We personally feed a balanced, fresh, raw diet made from chicken breast, thighs, necks, livers, hearts, and gizzards that follows an 80/10/10 ratio of muscle, bone and organs. When we initially began with this breed, we tried countless commercial brands, and many caused loose stool in young kittens. Once we began feeding a fresh, balanced raw diet, we significantly noticed improvement in their body condition, growth rate, stool consistency, and overall health.*
>
> JESSICA PETRAS
> *Liberty Bengals*

Your Bengal's ideal diet should consist mostly of animal-based ingredients. Cats are obligate carnivores, which means they must consume meat to survive. Vegetarian and vegan diets do not provide the necessary nutrients and are not recommended. Although some plant-based nutrients can be digested by cats, their gastrointestinal systems have not evolved to efficiently digest large quantities of plant-based carbohydrates.

Although cats and dogs are often thought to have similar dietary needs, this is one of the main differences between the two. Although dogs will not thrive on a plant-based diet, their digestive systems can handle carbohydrates more efficiently. Cats, on the other hand, must have a diet consisting mainly of animal-based products. Additionally, cats differ from dogs in that they cannot produce taurine within their own bodies. This important amino acid, which is commonly found in meat, must be consumed in their food. Taurine deficiency can cause serious health problems, including retinal degeneration, abnormal growth and development, and cardiomyopathy. For this reason, it's important to make sure you're feeding your Bengal a diet specifically formulated for cats. If you have a dog in your home, you may notice your cat eating some of his food, but it's important to provide your Bengal with his own food to ensure that he is getting the correct balance of essential nutrients.

Commercial Diets

> *Bengals (and cats in general) don't experience thirst like we do; they absorb most of their water from the food they ingest. Bengals do best on a raw food diet, but at the least we recommend a canned wet food. They seem to experience more bowel and litter box issues when on a dry food diet alone.*
>
> RENEE RORAGEN
> *The Rhine Bengals*

Dry cat food, or kibble, is the most common type of commercially produced cat food. Its popularity is due to its convenience and the fact that it can be found nearly everywhere. Kibble can be quite inexpensive and can be found not only in pet stores but in grocery and convenience stores as well. Kibble can be found in a wide range of formulas, varying in both quality and ingredients. Different formulas are also available to suit cats with specific needs such as age, food sensitivities, and health conditions.

Canned or wet food is another popular choice among cat owners. Like kibble, it's easy to find, store, and feed. Canned food is a great choice for picky cats, as many find it more palatable than dry food. Since it has a higher moisture content, wet food is also ideal for cats who don't drink enough water on their own. However, it does tend to stick to the teeth more than dry food, so a cat that only eats canned food may require more frequent dental care.

Fresh-cooked cat food is rising in popularity and is commonly found in the refrigerated section of your local pet store as well as in some grocery stores. There are also a number of companies that can ship your cat's food directly to you. Fresh cat food is generally packaged in either a roll or patty and must be cut into your cat's portion size. Fresh food typically consists of cooked meat, organs, and some fruits, vegetables, or other supplements. Many are free from preservatives and artificial ingredients. Unlike kibble, it must be stored in the refrigerator and can expire within a few days or weeks. Some fresh food can also be frozen for storage. Fresh food is typically somewhat expensive, especially if you have it shipped to your door, but it's a great option for finicky felines.

Another option rising in popularity among cat owners is the commercially available raw diet. More cat owners are seeking natural and species-appropriate diets for their cats but without the hassle of making it at home. Commercial raw diets can be found in the frozen section of your local pet store. Raw food is often packaged as a roll or patties and can be thawed and divided into smaller portions if necessary. This diet typically consists of a nutritionally balanced combination of muscle meat, organ, bone, and some fruits, vegetables, or added nutrients. Raw diets generally do not contain any grains, and many boast that they are free from artificial ingredients as well. A variety of protein choices is often available to suit different preferences or sensitivities. Since raw cat

food contains raw meat, it must be stored in the freezer. However, most cats prefer it thawed to room temperature. Raw food is not inexpensive, so if you are on a budget, you may need to consider other options. Additionally, there is some risk with handling raw meat, so it's important to follow proper hygiene and cleaning protocols. This is especially true for households with immunocompromised family members.

Homemade Diets

There are a number of reasons why you may consider making your Bengal's food at home. Making your own cat food will ensure that you know exactly what your cat is eating and will eliminate the possibility of your cat consuming allergens and subpar ingredients. However, it can be both time-consuming and expensive. It's also crucial to make sure you are feeding your cat a balanced diet. Commercial cat food is required by law to meet certain nutritional standards, but you will be on your own with a homemade diet. In order to ensure that you are making a nutritionally balanced diet, it's recommended that you work with a veterinary nutritionist. As stated earlier in the chapter, the ACVN website has a list of nutritionists on their website. The ACVN is an American organization, but their list contains the contact information for nutritionists around the world.

When making your cat's food, you'll first need to decide whether you intend to feed him a raw or cooked diet. You may combine these diets as needed,

FUN FACT
Predator Instinct

Owning a Bengal cat can be an adventure. These cats possess a strong hunting instinct and might surprise you with "gifts" such as small toys or even creatures they catch. Handling a Bengal cat's hunting instinct requires understanding and providing appropriate outlets for their natural behavior. For example, engaging in interactive play sessions with toys that mimic prey can help satisfy these instincts. In addition, providing environmental enrichment during mealtimes, such as puzzle toys or treat-dispensing toys, can stimulate your Bengal's mind and redirect its prey drive.

but it's important to note that while raw bones are safe for consumption, cooked bones are not. Cooked bones can splinter and seriously injure your cat. Although most cats can handle raw bones well, you may also consider using a meat grinder or a powdered calcium supplement. If you are feeding a cooked diet, you will need to use ground eggshells or another type of calcium supplement rather than bones. The feline nutritionist you choose will be able to recommend the best ingredients for your cat's unique needs.

It's important to note that with a meat-based homemade diet, you must remember to follow safety guidelines for handling raw meat. As they are obligate carnivores, the digestive systems of cats have evolved to handle small amounts of common pathogens. A healthy cat can consume a small amount of salmonella without issue, but a human cannot. You must be careful to clean properly and avoid contaminating the rest of your home while preparing your cat's food.

Some cats like to carry their food around, but if you are feeding a raw diet, you'll need to restrict his movement to a small, easy-to-clean area. Carpeted and fabric surfaces are difficult to properly sanitize, so try to keep your cat's food away from them. A silicone mat is a great option that can be easily wiped down or tossed in the dishwasher after use. If you are worried about pathogens, you may also want to wipe down your Bengal's face and paws after each meal.

Ingredients to Avoid

> **"**
>
> *I recommend Bengal owners avoid feeding any commercial cat food that has vegetables, grains, fruits, and glutens in it. You want a high-quality, high-protein food that has mostly meat ingredients. The first five ingredients on a cat food label should be meat ingredients. That will ensure it's a good meat-based diet.*
>
> TRACY WILSON
>
> *Wildtrax*
>
> **"**

If you choose to make your Bengal's food at home, it's important to be aware of what ingredients are safe for consumption. Certain amounts of toxic ingredients can cause serious health problems, including gastrointestinal distress and even death. If you like to share your snacks with your cat, you'll also need to be aware that some human foods can also be toxic. If you are worried that your Bengal may have consumed something toxic, call your veterinarian or local emergency veterinary clinic right away.

Common foods that are toxic to cats include:

- Onions
- Garlic
- Chocolate
- Caffeine
- Grapes & raisins
- Meat with seasoning or spices

Although animal-based ingredients are generally safe, large amounts can cause digestive upset, especially if the cat is not used to eating them. Fat and organ meat, for example, are generally safe in small amounts but can cause diarrhea or vomiting in large amounts. For this reason, it's important to stick closely to any recipes given to you by your feline nutritionist.

Weight Management

> "
>
> *Spaying and neutering contributes to obesity in cats. This is a fact that needs to be acknowledged. Intact cats are leaner and more muscular than spayed/neutered cats. It's an inconvenient truth. Unfortunately, at this time, there are no other alternatives for spaying/neutering. It is a necessary evil. Intact cats are very diffi-cult to live with, and most people cannot handle them. They spray, fight, and they are very loud. If you have a spayed/neutered cat (which most people do), the best thing you can do to keep the cat fit is to feed it high-quality protein (cooked, boneless, skinless chick-en), high-quality canned and dry cat food, and provide plenty of opportunities to exercise.*
>
> ERIN H.
>
> *Sarasota Bengals*
>
> "

A study performed in 2018 by the Association for Pet Obesity Prevention found that around half of all pet cats in the US were considered either overweight or obese. Of those cats, many owners were not able to recognize that their cats were not at a healthy weight. Additionally, many cat owners are undereducated about the detrimental effects that excess weight can have on their feline companions.

Although Bengals are considered a medium to large breed, there is no specific weight range. A healthy weight for one Bengal may be considered unhealthy for another. Rather than aiming for a specific weight, it's recommended to monitor your Bengal's body condition. When viewed from above, a healthy Bengal will have a visible waist. Looking at the cat from the side, the stomach should have a visible tuck up behind the ribs, though some cats may have a more prominent primordial pouch than others. Your Bengal's ribs should not be visible but must be easily felt. If you are not able to determine whether your Bengal is a healthy weight, ask your veterinarian at your next appointment.

There are two key aspects of weight management: portion control and exercise. While it's important to monitor your cat's meal sizes, you will also need to consider any snacks or treats your Bengal gets during a normal day. Those training sessions are great but don't forget to count those training treat calories. If your Bengal could lose a little weight, it's recommended to reduce his daily calorie intake. This can be accomplished through portion reduction or a change in diet. There are a number of low-calorie cat foods available to choose from. A lower-calorie food can help reduce your cat's daily calorie

intake without reducing the amount of food he gets, which can leave him hungry and irritable. If you are feeding your Bengal a commercial diet, the packaging likely provides feeding guidelines that can be adjusted to suit your cat's needs. Again, if you have any questions about portion size, ask your veterinarian or veterinary nutritionist.

It's also important to keep your Bengal active each day. Most Bengals enjoy physical activity and do not have a problem staying active. Remember, the more exercise your cat gets each day, the more calories he can consume. If you are worried about cutting your cat's portion sizes, you may need to compensate by increasing exercise. However, it's important to start slow if your Bengal has not been previously active. Like people, your cat will need to build fitness over time. You may need to start out with short play sessions and build duration as your Bengal gains fitness. Obesity can seriously affect a cat's mobility, so as your cat loses weight, you'll likely notice that he will be more interested in play and other physical activities.

CHAPTER 11

Your Bengal's Health Care

Choosing a Vet

After you've brought your Bengal home, it's recommended to schedule a check-up with a veterinarian. In fact, if you've purchased your Bengal from a breeder, you may be required to have a vet examine the kitten within a few days of bringing him home. If you have other pets at home already, you may already have a veterinarian in

mind. If not, you'll need to research local vets to find one you like. It can take some time to find the right clinic, but it will be worth it to know your beloved cat will receive the right care.

If you live near your Bengal's breeder, you may be able to ask for a recommendation. Taking your new cat to a vet familiar with the breed is great, but the added benefit is that the vet will likely have provided care for your kitten since birth. If you purchased your Bengal from a local rescue organization, they may also be able to recommend a veterinary clinic. Additionally, you can always ask the cat lovers in your life where they take their own companions for veterinary care.

The majority of small animal veterinary clinics care for both cats and dogs, but depending on where you live, you may be able to find a cat-only clinic. Feline-specific veterinary clinics are ideal for nervous cats, as you won't have to worry about barking dogs in the waiting room. The staff are also more familiar with feline care.

It can be easy to overlook, but you'll need to consider your schedule when searching for a new vet. Some clinics are only open during business hours from Monday through Friday, so if you work during those hours, you will need to take time off for any appointments. Some clinics may also be open during the evening hours or on weekends, so you should try to find a facility that can accommodate your schedule. Your area may also have a 24-hour clinic, which is ideal should your Bengal have a medical emergency. However, many emergency clinics do not provide routine care, so it's important to verify not only the hours of operation but the type of care provided as well. If a clinic only offers emergency care, it may still be worth your time to save their information if your cat needs care and your regular vet is closed.

If you are unable to obtain a recommendation, you can also consult the internet. The American Veterinary Medical Association (AVMA) and American Association of Feline Practitioners (AAFP) are great places to search. If you are interested in more holistic veterinary care, you can also check out the American Holistic Veterinary Medical Association (AHVMA). All of these websites have directories on their websites that are searchable by location as well as species and treatment type.

Regular Vet Visits

> *Bengals can develop heart and hip issues in their old age. Yearly check-ups with your vet can catch those problems early so they can be managed properly and give your cat a much better quality, and in some cases, quantity of life.*
>
> ELIZABETH NOLTE
> *Southern Pines Bengals*

Although many owners believe that it's a waste of money to take their cats to the vet when nothing is wrong, routine check-ups are crucial. Most vets recommend routine exams every six to 12 months for a healthy adult cat, but cats with health problems may need to be seen more frequently. At a minimum, you should plan on taking your Bengal to the vet at least once per year.

Although you will be able to monitor your Bengal's health at home, sometimes it can be difficult to see any small changes, especially if they happen over a long period of time. Your vet will have notes from every visit and will be able to pinpoint any changes in your cat's health. For example, it can be difficult for some owners to notice their cat's weight gain, but the vet will be able to tell you exactly how much weight your Bengal has gained and how to address the issue. Additionally, if you have any small concerns that don't warrant a vet visit on their own, routine exams can give you the opportunity to ask questions and express concerns.

Regular vet visits are also a great opportunity to keep track of your Bengal's dental care. Many owners do not regularly check their cat's mouth at home, but your vet will do so during a routine exam. If your Bengal's teeth have a buildup of plaque and tarter, you may need to schedule a dental cleaning. Depending on your Bengal's diet and overall health, he may need dental cleanings as often as once or twice per year. Additionally, if he is experiencing any dental issues, your vet may recommend at-home dental care or a change in diet or lifestyle.

Photo Courtesy of
Danielle Johnson

Your Bengal will also need to be kept up to date on all vaccinations and deworming, especially if he spends any time outside. Vaccines will be discussed later in the chapter, but some will need to be updated yearly, while others will only need to be done every few years. Again, your cat's specific vaccination schedule will depend on his health and the recommendations of your veterinarian.

Microchipping

Depending on where you purchased your Bengal cat, he may already have been implanted with a microchip. If he does not yet have a microchip, you'll need to mention it to your veterinarian at your next visit. Microchips are essential for all cats, regardless of whether they are allowed outdoors. You never know when your Bengal might slip through an open door, and without a collar and ID tag, it will be difficult or even impossible to be reunited with him. Microchips ensure that you can be contacted in the event that your Bengal is found by a kind stranger.

The microchip that will be implanted in your Bengal is about the size of a grain of rice. It is inserted by needle just beneath the skin above the shoulder blades. When the microchip is scanned with a microchip reader device, the microchip's unique number will appear on the screen. That number can then be searched in a database, and your contact information can be found.

Microchipping is a safe procedure, though some cats may experience minor discomfort during the insertion process. There are generally no side effects, though some cats may experience microchip migration, which is when the chip moves to another part of the body. This is somewhat common, so most shelters and clinics will scan the whole body if nothing shows up near the shoulder blades. If your cat has had a microchip for many years, there is a small possibility that it may not work properly for such a long period of time. For this reason, it's recommended to check the microchip at your Bengal's routine exams to make sure the chip still functions as intended. If not, a new microchip can be inserted.

Although microchips sound like expensive technology, the procedure is typically quite inexpensive. The cost will depend on the specific brand of microchip used as well as your location. In some cases, the cost to register the chip with the company will be covered by your vet bill, but you may need to pay the company directly. Fortunately, registration is generally less than $30. If you are on a budget, you may also be able to find low-cost microchipping events at a local vet clinic or shelter.

After your Bengal has been microchipped, it is your responsibility to make sure your contact information is updated each time anything changes. If your address or phone number is changed and you do not update the information, you may not be able to be contacted if your lost cat is found.

Additionally, if you plan on traveling internationally with your Bengal, it's important to make sure that his microchip is the appropriate type. There are many brands of microchips on the market, but not all are internationally accepted. A 15-digit ISO-compatible microchip is the international standard, so it's important to make sure your Bengal has the right chip to avoid travel complications. Many microchips in the US are 9- or 10-digit chips and will not be able to be read by customs agents in your destination country. If your Bengal already has a 9- or 10-digit chip, you can have a second chip implanted without a problem.

Photo Courtesy of Sabrina Lawson

Vaccinations

Your Bengal will receive multiple vaccines throughout his life to ensure that he is protected against common diseases. Those vaccines are typically categorized as either core or non-core vaccines. Core vaccines are recommended for all cats and are sometimes even required by law. With the exception of rabies, core vaccines are also commonly combined into a single syringe to avoid multiple injections. Non-core vaccines protect against less common diseases and are generally recommended on a case-by-case basis.

The American Association of Feline Practitioners (AAFP) recommends the following five core vaccines for every cat:

- Feline panleukopenia virus (FPV)
- Feline viral rhinotracheitis (FHV-1)
- Feline caliciviruses (FCV)
- Feline leukemia virus (FeLV)
- Rabies virus

Feline panleukopenia virus can cause severe and sometimes fatal infections in the stomach and intestines. This is a highly contagious disease that can spread quickly, so vaccination is essential.

Feline viral rhinotracheitis and **feline caliciviruses** can affect cats separately, but they also can occur together. Though rarely fatal, these viruses cause upper respiratory infections and can cause long-term health issues.

Feline leukemia virus is a highly contagious and widespread virus that damages the immune system and can cause tumors. The symptoms do not always appear right away, so some cats may be infected for a while before becoming ill. For this reason, some vets may require a blood test before vaccinating the cat.

Rabies is typically the only vaccine that is required by law in some areas. This is because it is a serious virus that can affect many species, including humans. Unfortunately, once the neurological symptoms of the disease appear, there is a 99.9% chance of fatality.

Common non-core vaccines recommended for cats include:

- Chlamydophila felis
- Bordetella brochiseptica
- Feline infectious peritonitis (FIP)

Chlamydophila felis causes feline chlamydiosis, also known as chlamydial conjunctivitis. It's common in all areas but frequently wreaks havoc in feral cat colonies. The disease causes upper respiratory infections, infertility in female cats, and painful swelling of the membranes around the eyes.

Bordetella is highly contagious and can spread quickly among groups of cats. It is rarely fatal, but the upper respiratory infection it causes can take several weeks to resolve under a veterinarian's care.

If you've brought home a Bengal kitten, he has likely already received his first vaccine between the ages of six and eight weeks. Following that initial dose, most vets recommend booster shots every four weeks until the kitten is 16 to 20 weeks. Adult cats will also need booster shots on occasion, but the exact schedule will depend on your vet's recommendation. High-risk animals may require yearly vaccinations, while low-risk cats may be able to go as long as three years between vaccinations.

Vaccine reactions are incredibly rare but not impossible. It's normal for some cats to seem a bit lethargic or have a low appetite for 24 to 48 hours post-vaccination. If your Bengal experiences vomiting, diarrhea, or difficulty breathing, contact your veterinarian as soon as possible.

Parasite Prevention

For indoor-only cats, parasite prevention is easy. However, if your Bengal spends much time outside, he will need to be on a regular preventive routine. External parasites, such as fleas and ticks, are easy for most owners to spot, but internal parasites, such as worms, will likely need to be diagnosed by your veterinarian. During your Bengal's annual check-up, your vet may ask to perform a fecal exam to test for internal parasites. Although it's common for dogs to undergo regular blood tests

HEALTH ALERT
Identifying Progressive Retinal Atrophy (PRA)

Progressive retinal atrophy (PRA) is a genetic condition that can affect Bengal cats' vision over time. To identify PRA, owners should watch for signs such as night blindness or difficulty seeing in dim light. Regular veterinary check-ups with thorough examinations are crucial for the early identification of this disease. While there is no known cure for PRA, preventative measures include responsible breeding practices and genetic testing. PRA treatment options are limited, but supportive care and environmental modifications can help affected cats adapt to their vision loss.

for heartworms, it's not generally recommended for cats. However, your vet may recommend monthly heartworm prevention, depending on where you live.

The most common intestinal worms are roundworms, tapeworms, and hookworms. Cats may also be infected with protozoa, such as toxoplasma, giardia, and isospora. Outdoor cats are more prone to parasitic infections because they are at a higher risk of ingesting infected food, water, soil, or feces. The most common external parasites are fleas and ticks, which are typically picked up by walking through infested grass or brush.

A cat with intestinal parasites may display symptoms such as lethargy, diarrhea, excessive gas, or sudden weight loss. A heavy parasitic load can also cause the cat to appear malnourished, with a distended belly. Heartworm causes slightly different symptoms, and infected cats may experience coughing, rapid breathing, vomiting, and weight loss.

Fortunately, intestinal parasites are relatively easy to treat with oral medication. The type of medication and length of treatment varies by parasite. Some infections may be resolved with a single dose, while others may require weeks of daily medication. Heartworm treatment can take several months, and physical activity must be limited due to the risk of blockage in major blood vessels as the parasites die off. However, most cats can recover from parasitic infections with few long-term issues.

Spaying and Neutering

> 66
>
> *Bengals tend to sexually mature faster than other breeds, and it is highly recommended to arrange their spay/neuter as soon as possible. Both intact male and female Bengal cats, as early as four months of age, can spray urine on a daily basis around the home. However, this can be completely avoided if your kitten is altered prior to hormone development.*
>
> JESSICA PETRAS
> *Liberty Bengals*
>
> 99

To prevent unwanted litters, bad behavior, and potential health problems, it's recommended to have your Bengal spayed or neutered at an appropriate age. Female cats are spayed, which is the name given to the surgical procedure where the ovaries and uterus are removed. Male cats undergo neutering, where their testicles are surgically removed. Unless you intend to show your Bengal in championship classes or start your own breeding program, spaying and neutering are recommended for a number of reasons. If showing is your only goal, you can still show an altered cat in premiership or household pet classes, which will be discussed in more detail in a later chapter.

Spaying and neutering can have a significant impact on a cat's behavior since hormones contribute to urine marking, aggression, and roaming. Surgical alteration can reduce or eliminate the behavior entirely, as well as prevent uterine infections, prostate issues, and several types of cancer. Unwanted litters contribute to the overpopulation of shelters and rescues but are entirely preventable by spaying and neutering cats not intended for ethical breeding programs.

Seven months is the most common age recommended for spaying and neutering, but your vet will be able to give a more accurate recommendation for your Bengal based on his overall health and body condition. Problem behaviors typically start to appear as a cat reaches sexual maturity, so most vets will typically recommend surgery before those problems develop.

Both spaying and neutering are safe procedures that are performed by vets nearly every day. Complications are rare so long as at-home care instructions are followed carefully. Your Bengal may be a bit less energetic for a few days, but recovery time is typically around 10 to 14 days. If you are concerned about anesthesia or any aspect of the surgery, don't be afraid to discuss your concerns with your vet. As your cat's advocate, it's important that you feel comfortable with his treatment.

If you intend to breed your Bengal, it's recommended to discuss the matter with your cat's breeder. Ethical breeding guidelines should always be followed to ensure that you are preserving the best qualities of the breed. Your breeder may be able to mentor you or recommend a mentor who will help you to develop an ethical and high-quality breeding program. Remember, breeding can risk the health and life of your cat, so it's important to consider this decision carefully and make sure you're doing it right.

Declawing

> 66
>
> *Do not ever declaw a Bengal! You can trim the nails; however, I just let them use the scratching post to file the claws down naturally*
>
> KRISTI HILDEBRAND
> *Mid Atlantic Bengals*
>
> 99

Although declawing is legal in much of the US, an increasing number of vets are unwilling to perform the procedure. In some European countries, it has even been outlawed due to the belief that it is cruel and unnecessary to remove a cat's claws. Since declawing involves the surgical amputation of the claws as well as the toe bones to which they are attached, it is considered a major surgical procedure. Declawing can cause emotional stress and affect the cat's ability to climb and balance itself. There are few studies that show increased problem behaviors in declawed cats. Additionally, declawing removes the cat's main form of defense, which can be a serious risk if the cat is allowed outdoors.

Scratching is a normal behavior for cats, but in some cases, it can become a destructive behavioral problem. If you are considering declawing your Bengal, it's recommended to talk to a feline behaviorist first. He or she may be able to provide guidance on how to manage or correct your cat's bad habits. You may also want to consider more humane options, such as frequent nail trims or nail caps.

Common Genetic Conditions

Overall, Bengals are a healthy breed, and ethical breeders are continually working to reduce and, hopefully, someday eliminate genetic health problems. However, there are a few issues that are prevalent in Bengals, including hypertrophic cardiomyopathy (HCM) and polycystic kidney disease (PKD).

HCM affects cats of all breeds, not just Bengals. In fact, it's the most common cardiac condition in cats of any breed. Affected cats suffer from a thickened heart wall, which reduces the heart's ability to pump blood effectively. As a result of poor blood circulation, affected cats are at a much higher risk of developing blood clots.

Cats affected by HCM may display symptoms such as shortness of breath, open-mouth breathing, appetite loss, lethargy, and weight loss. Unfortunately, HCM is incurable, but symptoms can be managed with medication and oxygen therapy. Once symptoms are present, however, the progression of the disease cannot be prevented.

PKD is a genetic disease that causes cysts in the cat's kidneys. In many cases, the cysts are present in the kidneys from birth and just grow larger over time. The cysts will eventually disrupt the organ's function, and kidney failure will occur. Not all cats will develop symptoms at the same age, but most are not affected until around seven years of age.

Cats affected by PKD will show symptoms such as excessive water intake and urination, nausea, vomiting, weight loss, lethargy, and a decrease in appetite. PKD is typically treated the same way as chronic kidney disease. Treatment may include oral medication, prescription diets, and fluid therapy. It's also important to note that not all cats affected with PKD will display symptoms. Some cats may experience slow-growing cysts and live their entire life without complications. However, since PKD is a genetic disorder, affected cats should not be bred to avoid passing the condition on to future generations. DNA testing can reveal whether or not a cat is afflicted with either PKD or HCM.

Photo Courtesy of
Lisa Ferrigno

Pet Insurance

As with human medical care, the cost of veterinary care continues to rise. As a result, pet insurance policies are becoming increasingly popular among pet owners. More companies are offering policies in a range of prices and coverage to suit pets of all breeds and ages. If you are interested in getting pet insurance for your Bengal, it's important to do your research before making a purchase. Not all policies offer the same coverage, and some do not cover older cats or those with preexisting conditions.

It's also important to be aware that most policies have waiting periods before coverage kicks in. Coverage may also vary by condition. For example, accidental injuries are often covered seven to 10 days after purchase, but the waiting period may be as long as 14 days or more for illnesses. Orthopedic conditions can have waiting periods of up to 30 days or more. If your Bengal suffers from an injury or illness before the waiting period is over, treatment will not be covered by your policy.

Young and healthy cats are the least expensive to insure, so it's generally better to buy a policy long before you may need it. That way, as your Bengal ages and develops health problems or injuries, you can be sure that his treatment will be covered.

However, the cost of monthly premiums can add up if you have a healthy cat. Rather than spending that money on insurance, some owners opt to put that money aside each month to save for a rainy day. Since most cats do not develop serious health problems until they reach their senior years, those savings can add up to enough to cover treatment. Plus, you won't need to negotiate coverage with an insurance company each time you take your cat to the vet. Before committing to an insurance policy, it's best to consider all of your options and whether pet insurance is right for you and your Bengal.

CHAPTER 12

Traveling with Your Bengal

Car Travel

> "
>
> *We have traveled across half the country with our cats. Bengals can be fantastic travel companions. We recommend a large travel carrier that can fit a small litter box and a bed. Bring a blanket to cover the cat if you find it is stressed, which is usually indicated by constant vocalization. Covering the cat makes a den, which allows it to feel safe, although this isn't necessary for all cats. Unless your Bengal is harness-trained and used to traveling, for its own safety, do not release your cat from the carrier. This prevents it from darting from the car, getting trapped under seats, or risking injury in the event of a car accident.*
>
> RENEE RORAGEN
> *The Rhine Bengals*
>
> "

Not all cats enjoy traveling with their owners, but some learn to enjoy spending time with their owners away from home. However, a successful road trip with your Bengal will require plenty of planning and preparation before your departure day. If you intend to travel with your cat frequently, you may even want to begin getting him used to the experience as soon as possible.

To begin preparing your Bengal for car travel, you'll first want him to get used to spending time in his carrier. Initially, this can be as easy as setting the open carrier out in the house and encouraging him to spend time inside. Make the carrier as inviting as possible, with comfortable bedding and perhaps a few treats. Once he's comfortable inside the carrier, you can try closing the door and walking around the room with the carrier in your arms or over your shoulder, depending on

FUN FACT
World Record Duo

In 2021, an adorable Bengal cat and Boston Terrier duo captivated the world with a unique set of skills: riding a scooter. This pair, comprised of seven-year-old Sashimi the cat and five-year-old Lollipop the dog, broke the Guinness World record for the fastest five meters on a scooter by a dog and cat pair. Sashimi and Lollipop managed this feat in 4.37 seconds. This Bengal cat and Boston Terrier live with their owner, Melissa Millett, in Ontario, Canada.

the style. If your cat seems comfortable, you can venture outside. As you progress, you can put the carrier in the car and try driving around the block. Remember to provide your Bengal with plenty of praise and a few treats. However, if your Bengal has a tendency to get carsick, you may want to refrain from the treats.

When traveling by car, it's never recommended to allow your Bengal to ride unrestrained. A loose cat can be a danger to you, your passengers, and anyone else on the road. If your cat were to get scared, he could potentially jump on you and distract you from your driving. In the unfortunate event of an accident, an unrestrained cat could also escape from the car and run into traffic. For these reasons, the safest option is acclimating your Bengal to his carrier. Ideally, you should also secure the carrier in the car using a seat belt or straps. This will prevent the carrier from bouncing around the car should you have an accident or even just have to make a hard stop or turn.

If your trip is more than a few hours, you may want to consider providing your Bengal with a travel litter box. If his carrier can't fit a small box, you can always set one up on the floor of the car or in the cargo area. If the box is outside the carrier, you can give your cat a bathroom break whenever you need one for yourself. Just make sure that all doors and windows are secure before letting your Bengal loose in the car. These breaks are also a great opportunity to offer water so that your cat doesn't become dehydrated. If possible, it's recommended to use the same litter as you do at home to encourage normal bathroom habits.

For easy clean-up, consider using litter-box liners or disposable puppy pads. Puppy pads can also be used to line your Bengal's carrier to make clean-up easier if he has an accident or gets carsick. It can be helpful to bring a few with you, so have spares if needed, as well as a disposable plastic bag so that you can dispose of any soiled pads or used litter.

When traveling with your Bengal, you'll also want to remember to bring all necessities from home. Unless your cat is an experienced traveler, having the same items as you do at home can help put him at ease and make the trip less stressful. As mentioned previously, using the same litter can help your cat feel more comfortable using the litter box. It's also recommended to continue feeding the same type of food as you do at home. Some cats may prefer to drink water from home, so if your Bengal is picky about what he drinks, you may need to bring a container of water with you. Don't forget to bring a bed or blanket from home as

well. If you're embarking on a lengthy trip, you may also want to bring grooming supplies and toys.

Finally, if you are taking your Bengal by car to another state or country, don't forget to check the legal requirements for traveling with pets to your destination. It's always recommended to bring your cat's vaccination records with you, but you may also be required to have a health certificate from your vet or other health information. You won't always be asked to show documentation, but it's better to be prepared just in case.

> "
> *Please make sure your carrier is large enough so the cat can sit up, stretch out, and turn around. I see so many people put their cats in carriers that are way too small. Always secure the carrier with a seat belt or other device so it doesn't move around while driving. Cats can get scared in the car, so I recommend you do not take the cat out of the carrier while in the car. I use Feliway wipes on the carrier to calm the cat. Feliway is a pheromone product that calms cats down.*
>
> ERIN H.
> *Sarasota Bengals*
> "

Air Travel

As with car travel, if you intend to travel by air with your Bengal, you'll need to begin preparing for your trip far in advance. Again, acclimating your cat to his carrier is key, and the process should begin as soon as possible. You'll also want to book your Bengal's airfare when you purchase your own tickets. Most flights have restrictions on the number of pets allowed, so it's important to book it as soon as possible. Depending on the flight, you may have the choice of having your cat travel in the cabin with you or in cargo. If you want your Bengal to travel in-cabin, you'll need to choose an appropriate seat, as pets are not permitted in exit rows or against bulkheads.

With air travel, it's even more important to have your Bengal's travel documents, as many airlines will ask for proof of vaccination or health certifications. These documents are crucial if you are traveling internationally, as you will need to present them when you pass through customs. As previously mentioned, the required documents will vary by destination, so be sure to do your research before your trip so that you are adequately prepared.

If your Bengal is traveling in-cabin with you, you will need to take him through security. His carrier will need to be x-rayed, and you will be asked to carry him through the screening device. For your cat's safety, it's recommended to fit him with a comfortable harness and leash so that if he wiggles out of your arms, he will not be able to run off.

Travel can be stressful for many cats, but most veterinarians do not recommend sedation during flights. If you are worried, you may want to discuss the matter with your veterinarian. There are many nonpharmaceutical options on the market, including pheromone sprays that can help calm your Bengal without sedation. Additionally, the more comfortable your cat is in his carrier, the less stressed he will be during travel, so try to introduce it as early as possible.

As suggested for car travel, it's recommended to line your Bengal's air travel carrier with a disposable puppy pad. That way, if he has an accident or gets airsick, clean-up will be a breeze. Although it can be difficult to carry litter and food on an airplane, it's recommended to have at least a couple of days of food with you. If you run into any issues or delays, you won't need to worry about feeding your cat. Just remember that you will need to buy litter and any other necessary supplies when you reach your destination.

Cat-Friendly Accommodations

One of the most challenging aspects of traveling with cats is finding pet-friendly accommodations. Not all places allow pets, and many will charge an extra fee. However, many hotel chains are famously pet friendly, and it's entirely possible to find a place to stay if you do your research in advance.

If you are not interested in staying in a hotel, you may also want to explore short-term rentals or bed and breakfasts. Hotels can sometimes be a bit noisy, and that can make a nervous cat even more uncomfortable, so it's important to consider all options.

Wherever you choose to stay, remember to be a courteous guest. Allowing your Bengal to be messy or disruptive may cause the hotel or rental owner to change their pet policy, which will only make it more difficult to find pet-friendly accommodations in the future. You may need to put a little extra effort into keeping your Bengal entertained so that he isn't disruptive, and you must make sure to clean up all messes. However, traveling with pets rarely goes as planned, so if you run into any issues, try to be honest with your host and patient with your Bengal.

> *If you travel with your Bengal, you will need to make sure it is updated in its vaccines, including rabies. Also, you will want to have a copy of the pedigree on hand to show any customs officer that this is a Bengal cat and not a hybrid or early-generation Bengal, as lots of states/countries have banned these animals without a CITIES permit. If you have an official pedigree, you will avoid many of these issues.*
>
> MARIE-LISA LAROCQUE
> *MarieBengal*

Leaving Your Cat Behind

> *Check travel regulations before taking your Bengal to another state. Some states or regions still have restrictions and do not allow Bengals. Hawaii does not allow them at all. If you fly or use any other commercial transportation, your cat is required to have a health certificate, and if it is 12 weeks or older, a rabies vaccination is required in order to travel. You can be fined and have your pet confiscated and quarantined if you attempt to enter another country without a health certificate and/or an entry permit.*
>
> ELIZABETH NOLTE
> *Southern Pines Bengals*

If you would prefer to avoid the hassle of bringing your Bengal with you on your trip, you will need to make sure he's taken care of while you're away. Not all cats enjoy traveling, but there are many options to consider when leaving them behind. The most common choices are in-home pet sitters and boarding facilities. Some veterinary clinics also offer boarding, which is ideal for cats that require extra care, such as medication. You may also want to ask the cat lovers in your life if they would be willing to take care of your Bengal while you're away. Remember, the cost of pet sitters and boarding facilities can vary by location and the level of services offered. Additionally, many facilities fill up fast during certain times of the year, so it's important to plan ahead and book your cat's stay as early as possible.

If you intend to board your Bengal, you will likely be required to provide proof of vaccination. Some facilities may also require deworming or flea and tick prevention prior to dropping your cat off. Again, it's important to plan ahead so that you can make an appointment with your vet to have everything taken care of before your departure.

When researching boarding facilities, don't be afraid to ask for an in-person tour. Most facilities are happy to show potential clients the space where their pets will be staying. If the staff seems hesitant to show you around, you may want to keep looking for a facility with more transparency. Different facilities will also have different-sized spaces, and they may be priced accordingly. If you have multiple cats that you would like to stay together, you'll need to look for a place that is big enough to accommodate them. Some facilities may offer oversized kitty condos or even whole rooms, depending on your budget.

Some facilities board both cats and dogs, so you should be sure to verify that the cats are kept in a separate area from the dogs. Many cats can become stressed listening to barking all day, so if your Bengal is sensitive, you may want to look for a cat-only facility or one where the cats are kept in a quieter area away from the dogs.

While all boarding facilities will provide basic care, such as daily feeding and litter box cleaning, you may also ask about additional services. Many facilities offer a certain amount of time each day for cuddling and playtime, but some will charge extra. If your Bengal likes a lot of attention, you may consider paying for a bit of extra time each day, especially if you're going to be gone for a long time. If your Bengal is on medication, it may cost extra to have it administered, especially if it's injectable rather than oral.

As recommended earlier in the chapter, it's recommended to continue using the same food and litter while away from home. Although many boarding facilities offer to use their food and litter, your Bengal will be more comfortable using what he is used to. Be sure to bring bedding from home as well since the familiar items will help to minimize stress.

If your Bengal would prefer not to leave home at all, you can consider hiring an in-home pet sitter. You will likely have the option of drop-in or overnight visits. With drop-in visits, the sitter will stop by your home a certain number of times per day to provide basic care and attention. As the name suggests, an overnight sitter will stay in your home overnight. This is generally a better option for attention-hungry cats, but it is the more expensive option.

Many pet sitters will also offer additional services such as mail collection and plant care, which is ideal if you plan to be away for a long time. These types of sitters will help keep your home in good condition while

Photo Courtesy of Julie Filion

also deterring potential thieves that could be targeting empty houses in your area.

When searching for a pet sitter, it's recommended to look for one that is insured and has plenty of references. You should also find one that is willing to meet with you before your trip so that you can introduce them to your Bengal and get to know them better. It's important to find someone you trust so that you can travel without constantly worrying about your cat and your home. The meeting will also be a good opportunity to ask about the cost of basic care and any additional services you may be requesting.

Whether you choose to use a boarding facility, pet sitter, or friend, it's crucial that you leave emergency contact information. In addition to leaving your own contact information, whether phone or email, you should also leave the contact information of a trusted friend or family member. If you are unable to be contacted, the secondary emergency contact may be called. Additionally, you should also leave your vet's information, as well as any 24-hour emergency clinics in the area.

Remember, the more prepared you are for your trip, the better your Bengal will handle it. If you are stressed about leaving him behind, he will likely sense it and experience his own stress. This is why it's so important to find someone you trust. If you know that you are leaving your cat in good hands, you can both enjoy your vacations knowing you'll be reunited soon.

CHAPTER 13

Into the World of Showing

All About Cat Shows

C at shows aren't for everyone, but they are a fun and fulfilling experience for many purebred cat owners. If you've purchased a show-quality Bengal from a reputable breeder, you've already taken the first big step toward getting involved in the world of cat shows. As a purebred cat, your Bengal is likely already registered with

an organization such as the CFA or TICA, though there are other organizations as well. With your cat's registration documents in hand, you will also be able to register him with other associations. For example, if your Bengal already has CFA papers, it's a relatively simple process to register him with TICA. This means that you will then be able to show him at both CFA- and TICA-sanctioned cat shows. The Cat Fanciers' Federation (CFF) and American Cat Fanciers' Association (ACFA) also hold shows for cats registered with their organizations.

In general, cat shows are held on weekends so that they do not interfere with the typical workweek schedule. The average cat show will usually have several different show rings running at once, each with a different judge. The rings are judged independently, so the cat that wins in one ring may not win in another, depending on the judges' opinions. Cats can be entered in multiple rings, giving them multiple opportunities to bring home ribbons.

Despite the average person's first impression of cat shows, they are not judged according to which cat is the cutest. Each cat is carefully evaluated against its breed's written standard. Judges spend many years studying breed standards and are experts at recognizing the ideal characteristics of each breed. However, not all judges will interpret the breed standard exactly the same way, which is why there may be different results in different rings.

A cat will always be classified as one of two types: all-breed or specialty. As the name suggests, all-breed shows are open to all cat breeds, including mixed breeds or household cats. Specialty shows only allow cats of a specific type or coat length to compete. At an all-breed show, there will also be separate competitions for pedigreed purebred cats and household pets.

Any cat, including a rescue, can compete in the household pet category. If a purebred cat does not meet its breed standard, it may also compete in the household pet category. However, it's important to note that all cats competing in this category must be spayed or neutered by the age of eight months. Additionally, no cats are allowed to compete if they are declawed, though you may be required to trim your cat's claws prior to presenting him in the show ring.

The purebred cat category of competition is divided into three classes: kitten, championship, and premiership. Cats between the ages of four and eight months are entered into the kitten class, but all cats over the age of eight months must be entered into either championship or premiership. Championship classes are used by breeders as a way to evaluate their breeding stock, though not all competing cats will be bred. All cats competing in this class must be intact. If a cat has been spayed or neutered, it must be entered in the premiership class. It's not uncommon for cats to first be shown in championship classes, then later shown in premiership after they have been spayed or neutered.

All cats entered in competition will first compete against cats of the same breed, color, and gender. After competing against the same gender, cats will then compete against the opposite gender within the same breed and color. That winner is declared Best of Color and will go on to compete against other colors of the same breed. The winner of Best in Breed will then be evaluated against other breeds to win Best in Show. Best in Show is an incredibly prestigious title, as only one cat may win. The winner of Best in Show is determined by the judge as the cat that most closely resembles its breed standard.

Depending on the organization you choose to show with, you may also see agility competitions offered. If you are familiar with dog agility competitions, you will have some idea what this class is about. All cats, regardless of pedigree status, may compete. Agility competitions are not broken down by breed, so purebred and mixed breeds cats all have an equal chance at winning. The area is fully enclosed for safety, and the cats must complete an obstacle course in a certain amount of time. Each run is timed, and scores are given based on the number of obstacles completed successfully. The judge may also award bonus points if a cat is successful in completing the entire course under the maximum allotted time.

Though the handler is not permitted to touch the cat, a toy may be used to lure the cat through the obstacles. The obstacles typically consist of jumps, tunnels, weave poles, and more. They must be completed in a specific order set by the judge. Though agility classes are not available at all shows, they are a fun and challenging opportunity to spend time with your cat.

Bengal Breed Standards

The purpose of a breed standard is to describe an ideal example of the breed. No cat is perfect, but a breed standard gives purebred cat breeders a goal to work toward in their breeding program. When a breeder produces cats with the breed standard in mind, the result is consistency in type. Without a standard, breeders would produce cats with varying appearances, and breeds would change and disappear. The need to evaluate breeding stock is important, which is why reputable breeders choose to show their cats. Many people struggle to see the flaws in their own cats, so having the outside opinions of judges can help them determine which cats should be bred and which are better suited as pets only.

It should also be noted that even when breeders produce litters with the breed standard in mind, not all kittens will resemble the ideal Bengal. Even in a litter produced by two

FUN FACT
Breed Accepted Colors

According to TICA, there are several accepted colors and color patterns for Bengal cats. The primary breed-accepted colors are brown, silver, and seal. Within these colors are also accepted patterns, including Brown Tabby, Silver Tabby, Seal Lynx Point, Seal Mink Tabby, Seal Sepia Tabby, Marble, Spotted, Charcoal Spotted, and Charcoal Marble. The most common Bengal cat coloring is Brown Tabby or Brown.

champion Bengals, there may only be one or two show-quality kittens. The rest may be better suited as pets rather than for being shown and bred. If those kittens were to be bred, their future litters may be even further from ideal, diminishing the signature appearance of the Bengal.

The breed standard states that Bengal cats are medium to large, with a sleek and muscular build. Males are typically larger than females. When viewed from the side, the hindquarters are slightly higher than the shoulder.

The Bengal's head should be broad and wedge-shaped with high cheekbones. The markings and striking expression of the eyes give the breed a wild appearance. Mature male Bengals often have large jowls. The ears are medium to small with rounded tips. The Bengal's eyes should be round or oval with rich color. The color of the eye depends on the coat color but may be gold, green, aqua, or blue.

The body of a Bengal should always be long and substantial. Males tend to be more muscular than females, but all should have the appearance of a strong and athletic animal. Bengals are not delicate cats. The tail should be medium in length and tapered at the end with a rounded tip.

The coat is a signature characteristic of the breed. It is short, soft, and luxurious. Some Bengals may have "glitter," which is an iridescent shimmer. The coat pattern may be either rosetted or marbled. Coat colors vary in shade but are typically divided into four categories: brown, silver, snow, and blue. Bengals may also be semi-longhaired, and this variety is often called the Cashmere Bengal. A silky coat texture and glitter are highly desirable in the longhaired variety.

In the show ring, rosetted Bengals may be penalized for having vertical stripes resembling a mackerel tabby pattern. Marbled Bengals with circular bull's-eye patterning will also be faulted. Disqualifications in the breed include a belly without pattern, a kinked or deformed tail, cow hocks, and crossed eyes.

Getting Started in Cat Shows

> **"**
>
> *Bengals have an easy-to-care-for coat and do not normally need to be bathed. However, when we show our Bengals, we often use a high-quality degreasing shampoo about 24 to 48 hours before a show. We do not recommend conditioner, as this can weigh the coat down and cause excessive buildup.*
>
> JESSICA PETRAS
> *Liberty Bengals*
> **"**

If you are interested in showing your Bengal, your greatest resource will be the breeder you purchased your cat from. Even if your breeder is not local, he or she may know of other owners and breeders in your area that can help you get involved in cat shows. You should also consider attending a few cat shows as a spectator or volunteer before entering your first show. By watching and volunteering, you can better understand what you and your Bengal will need to do.

Additionally, many show organizations have volunteers or ambassadors who can provide information to newcomers and spectators alike. Many exhibitors are also happy to talk about showing, so long as you don't interrupt them on their way to the ring. Cat shows can be bustling places, so it's always best to ask if someone has time for questions. They may simply ask you to come back later when they are not in such a rush.

When attending a cat show, it's crucial that you understand that you are not allowed to touch any cat without the owner's permission. Many

Photo Courtesy of Melissa Johnson

exhibitors spend hours grooming their cats and may not want just any-one handling the animals. If you are told no, don't be offended. This same principle applies to photography, so be sure to ask the owner before taking any pictures of the cats.

Once you are ready to enter your Bengal in your first cat show, you'll need to fill out an entry form. The form will vary by organization, but you may need to fill it out online, in PDF form, or on paper. The information required will include your Bengal's registered name, registration num-ber, breed, sex, and coat color and pattern. If you are not entering the household pet category, the form may also ask for your Bengal's sire, dam, and breeder. You will also need to provide your own information, including your name, address, phone number, and email address. You also need to specify the class you intend to enter. Finally, the form will have a spot where you can make additional requests, such as an extra cage or grooming space—be aware that this may cost extra. After filling out the form completely, you'll need to pay your entry fees. The cost of your entry will depend on the organization you're showing with, as well as the specific classes you've entered.

Once you've received confirmation of your entry from show orga-nizers, you can begin gathering your supplies. Most shows will provide you with a cage and possibly a chair or two, but it's best to confirm this when you send in your entry. You will also want to ask about the size of the cage so that you can purchase appropriately sized "show curtains." These curtains are designed to cover the cage and provide your cat with a bit of privacy and comfort. However, if you are just starting out, a flat bedsheet will work too. It's common for cat show exhibitors to color coordinate their cat's show equipment, so you may want to match your show curtains to your cat's bedding or cage liner as well. The show you're attending may also have vendors, so you can always start simple and shop around for upgrades for your next show.

Your cat show supply list should include basic necessities such as a litter box, litter, food and water bowls, food and water, and fans if the weather is warm. It's also recommended to bring cleaning supplies, towels, and disposable bags so that you can clean up any accidents or messes. Don't forget to bring grooming supplies as well as anything you may need for yourself. Cat show days can be long, so bring plenty of food and water for yourself and any human companions. If the show orga-nizers are not providing chairs, consider bringing one or more folding chairs. You may also want to bring cash if you plan on shopping among the vendors or food stands.

On show day, you should plan to arrive at least an hour before judg-ing begins. That will ensure you have enough time to get settled. Your Bengal will be more comfortable in the show ring if you can arrive early enough for him to get used to the sights, smells, and sounds. If you arrive late and have to rush him into the ring, he may be stressed. For your first show, you want him to have a good experience, so try to plan ahead and be prepared.

When you first arrive, you'll need to check in with show officials. They'll give you the information you need to find your assigned cage. Once you locate your cage, you can get it set up for your Bengal and let him settle down inside. When you check in, you may also receive a show catalog, which is a list of all cats entered in the show. Each cat is assigned an entry number, so you'll need to check the catalog to find your Bengal's number. Remember that number, as it will be used to identify your cat

for the entire show. You'll also want to check the catalog for the judging schedule so you know when to present your Bengal and in which show ring. The classes will not be listed by time but rather by the order of judging. The only time listed in the catalog is the time judging begins, so it will be your responsibility to keep track of the show ring. By comparing the classes in the ring to the judging schedule in the catalog, you will be ready when your group is called to the ring.

When your group enters the show ring, you'll place your Bengal in the cage with his entry number on it. Make sure the door is latched securely, then find yourself a comfortable place to wait in the audience area. Cat shows do not require handlers, and owners do not take an active role in showing their cats. Instead, the judge will take each cat out individually for evaluation. The judge will announce the results, and the ring clerk will let you know when you may collect your cat. At that time, you'll also be able to collect any ribbons that have been won. If your Bengal placed well in his class, you might need to bring him back to the ring later so that he can compete against other groups of cats.

Most cat shows are two-day events, taking place on both Saturday and Sunday. When judging is over on Saturday afternoon, you may leave your cage set up for Sunday. This is common practice, and you do not typically have to worry about anyone taking your show curtains, bedding, or litter box. After judging on Sunday, you can clean up your area and make sure you have all of your belongings. Regardless of how well your Bengal did, don't forget to celebrate the experience and note what you might do differently next time. It can be easy to get caught up in the competition, but remember that showing should always be a fun bonding experience for you and your beloved Bengal.

CHAPTER 14

Your Aging Bengal Cat

Common Signs of Aging

> "
> *Bengals can live up to 20 years, but the average life span is 15 to 18 years for most. Older Bengals will have the same issues as any other elderly cats, such as diabetes if they are overweight or have kidney disease, heart disease, etc. Annual vet check-ups can detect these issues early so that they can be managed to help maintain the cat's quality of life.*
>
> TRACY WILSON
>
> *Wildtrax*
> "

Aging is a complex process, and not all cats will feel its effects the same way. Some cats may live well into their teens with the health of their youth, while others may begin experiencing the aches and pains of age much earlier. Cats are typically considered to have reached their senior years at around 11 years of age. Cats older than 15 are sometimes called super seniors because of their advanced age. Despite these general guidelines, it can be difficult to predict how and when your Bengal may begin showing his age.

One of the first signs of age shown by many cats is a loss of energy. You may not notice right away, as it can happen over time, but senior cats are typically far less active than young adults. Your senior Bengal may spend his time napping instead of racing around the house like he did in his youth. Unfortunately, a change in energy level can also result in weight gain, so you should expect to adjust your cat's diet as he ages. Some senior cats can also develop arthritis, which can affect their mobility. It's common for older cats to struggle with jumping or climbing onto high surfaces.

Some aging cats may also experience a loss of vision or hearing. If you notice your Bengal ignoring you more than usual or getting startled by your touch on occasion, it could be a decline in his sight or hearing. This

Photo Courtesy of Nina Peterson

is common, and most cats adapt well, but you must be prepared to adjust the way you interact with your cat to avoid accidentally frightening him.

Cognitive decline is also common in senior cats, and it can be difficult for many owners to manage. Some older cats may begin getting confused at times or have a difficult time navigating the home they once knew so well. Behavioral changes can also develop as a result of cognitive decline. You may notice your senior cat staring into space or at a wall for long periods of time or vocalizing for seemingly no reason. Some cats may also experience changes in their sleeping schedule, which can conflict with their owner's normal routine. Cognitive decline can also contribute to urinating or defecating outside of the litter box, though other health conditions may need to be ruled out first. If your Bengal begins to exhibit any alarming behavior, be sure to talk to your veterinarian as soon as possible.

Basic Senior Cat Care

> Regular vet visits are important. As your Bengal gets older, you should include blood work to make sure everything is functioning as it should be. If there is an issue, the blood work can detect it, and preventative measures can be put in place to ensure a long, healthy life.
>
> SHERYL KOONTZ
> *Marechal Cattery*

Comfort should always be your priority when caring for your aging Bengal. Aging cats may require certain accommodations in their home to prevent injury and discomfort, so be prepared to adjust your home and lifestyle if necessary. You may need to rearrange your furniture or provide your Bengal with different resting options. He may not be able to jump up into that sunny window anymore, so you may need to place his bed lower or provide him with pet stairs. If reaching your Bengal's litter box area involves navigating a flight of stairs, you may need to move it to a different level of your home. These small changes can have a big impact on your Bengal's quality of life, so it's important to take them seriously.

Additionally, your senior Bengal may require a different style of litter box or simply more litter boxes. Many older cats struggle to reach their litter box in time if they have to travel across the house or navigate high litter box walls. Large boxes with low sides are ideal for most senior cats.

As your Bengal reaches his senior years, your vet may also recommend more frequent routine exams. Most healthy adult cats can go a

Photo Courtesy of
Nina Peterson

year between check-ups, but many vets recommend that senior cats get checked at least every six months. If your Bengal has any chronic health conditions, he may need to be seen even more frequently. A senior cat's health can decline quickly, so it's important to catch any issues as soon as possible.

Self-grooming can also become a challenge for many older cats, so you may need to spend more time brushing your Bengal. Difficult-to-reach areas

FUN FACT
The Glitter Effect

Some Bengal cats have a glitter effect on their fur, creating the illusion of shimmering in some lighting conditions. Cats with this dazzling coat are often called Glitter Bengals and may have either mica or satin glitter coats. This unique effect is usually caused by a hollow area in their hair that catches the light and adds to their allure and beauty. Not all Bengal cats have a glitter coat, but this trait is considered highly desirable.

such as the back and hind end can become matted if your cat isn't grooming himself. Those mats can become painful if not addressed, so it may be best to schedule grooming sessions more often. Senior cats can also become more sensitive, so you may need to be more cautious about your handling and brushing techniques.

Photo Courtesy of Darlene J. Sato

Illness and Injury Prevention

> "
>
> *Some cats can have thyroid problems when they get older. It is important to have your cat checked out by a vet if you notice weight loss and changes in appetite. Hyperthyroidism can happen, and it is easily treated with medication.*
>
> ERIN H.
>
> *Sarasota Bengals*
>
> "

As previously mentioned, one of the best ways to keep your Bengal healthy as he ages is to monitor his health closely. More frequent check-ups with your vet are a great way to ensure that health problems are addressed quickly. If your cat takes medication regularly, he may require regular blood work to make sure his liver and kidneys are functioning well. Some medications may also require occasional adjustments in dosage, so frequent vet visits are a great way for your vet to monitor your Bengal's needs.

It's also important to note that many senior cats are unable to recognize their physical limitations at first. Your Bengal may no longer be able to leap great distances, but that doesn't mean he won't try. It will then become your responsibility to prevent his attempts by rearranging furniture or otherwise adjusting your home. You will not be able to prevent every illness or injury in your Bengal's life, but sometimes a few simple changes are all it takes to keep him as healthy and happy as possible.

FUN FACT
The Oldest Bengal Cat

Bengal cats are generally healthy and can enjoy a typical life span of 12 to 20 years. The oldest recorded Bengal cat reportedly reached the age of 34. While not every Bengal cat will reach such a remarkable age, providing them with a loving home, balanced diet, regular veterinary care, and plenty of opportunities for exercise can contribute to a long and happy life.

Traction can become a serious problem for many older cats as they lose the strength to keep their feet beneath them. If you have hardwood or tile floors in your home, you may begin noticing your Bengal slipping on occasion, especially as he attempts to jump. If there are certain areas your cat seems to struggle with, you may want to consider placing a rug or mat there to provide him with more traction. If you are using pet stairs or a ramp to provide your Bengal with accessibility, make sure they have nonslip surfaces such as carpet, turf, or rubber.

Remember, things can change quickly at this age, so if you notice any changes in your aging Bengal's health or behavior, it's important to contact your veterinarian.

Senior Cat Nutrition

> *Continue to love your senior Bengal as you have always loved it. Make sure you always provide yearly veterinary examinations. If anything out of the ordinary does come up, make sure you get the cat to the vet for a thorough examination. Oftentimes, when a cat begins to have a problem out of the ordinary, it has an underlying medical cause rather than just being a sudden behavioral issue. Bengals deserve a long-term, loving, and patient family that will give them all the care they need until the end!*
>
> RHEA SCHMITT
> *Bella Luna Gatte*

Although age affects cats differently, you can be certain that you will need to adjust your Bengal's diet at some point. Some cats may begin losing weight, while others may gain it. Rather than changing his food the moment he reaches a certain birthday, try to monitor your cat's body condition and adjust his diet accordingly.

Portion control is one of the easiest ways to manage a healthy weight. For senior cats that experience weight gain, you may need to reduce meal sizes. Free feeding is not recommended for any senior cat, as it can be impossible to closely monitor daily intake. Instead, you should plan on regular mealtimes with a specific portion for each meal. That way, you will know that your Bengal isn't overeating.

Photo Courtesy of Chuck & Tracy Fox

For senior cats that experience weight loss or a reduction in appetite, changing portion sizes will not have any effect. If your cat is not eating his food, there is no point in increasing the portion size. You may need to change or adjust his food instead. A more enticing food, such as canned, fresh, or raw food, can encourage a picky eater to eat more. You can decide whether to switch the food entirely or use a certain kind as a topper. A change in food can also be beneficial for overweight cats if you switch to a lower-calorie diet.

Many cat food companies manufacture senior formulas to meet the dietary needs of older cats. While foods intended for all life stages may be fine for some older cats, senior diets can provide many nutritional benefits, depending on the brand. Some senior cat foods contain more antioxidants to support aging immune systems, while others may simply be more digestible. Senior cat foods often have optimized calorie levels to help older cats maintain a healthy weight. Glucosamine and chondroitin are also common ingredients to help support healthy joints. Evaluating different foods can be overwhelming, so if you aren't sure what type of food to feed your senior Bengal, ask your veterinarian or veterinary nutritionist for advice.

CHAPTER 15

When It's Time to Say Goodbye

When to Say Goodbye

> "
>
> *Cats age faster than humans do, unfortunately. Just give them the love and affection they deserve in their old age. They may need more care, better food, or want to laze about more. Let them. Don't abandon them because they have become a burden. You are their life. Treat them how you would like to be treated in your old age. Be with them when they go over the rainbow bridge and be the last thing they see. I feel like we should always do that for any pet.*
>
> AMY CHASTAIN
>
> *BestBengals4u*
>
> "

Every cat owner dreads the day they must say goodbye to their beloved companion. The decision to say goodbye is difficult, but it is your responsibility to know when it's the right time. Remember, the kindest gift is to provide your Bengal with a peaceful and pain-free ending.

Many owners have a difficult time seeing through their grief. It can be easy to doubt yourself and your decision, so many veterinarians recommend using the H5M2 Quality of Life Scale. Dr. Alice Villalobos is the veterinary oncologist who developed the scale to help vets and owners know when it's time to say goodbye. Each of the seven categories is given a score of 0 to 10 points. If the overall score is below 35, humane euthanasia may be recommended. A score of 70 represents a perfect quality of life.

The categories of the H5M2 scale are as follows:

- **Hurt** – Consider your Bengal's daily pain level. Can it be kept under control with medication? Is he able to breathe without distress?

- **Hunger** – Evaluate your Bengal's appetite and his ability to eat. Is he able to maintain a healthy body condition? Can he eat without help, or must he be hand fed?

- **Hydration** – Does your Bengal drink enough water each day? Does he need subcutaneous fluids to maintain hydration? Using his current weight, calculate 10 ml per pound to determine an appropriate amount of water intake per day.

- **Hygiene** – Consider your Bengal's overall hygiene. Can he be kept clean and free from feces and other bodily fluids? Can he move or be moved enough to prevent sores?

- **Happiness** – Does your Bengal still enjoy his favorite activities? Is he interested in play or affection from his family, or is he depressed and unresponsive?

- **Mobility** – Is your Bengal able to move freely on his own, or is he at risk of stumbling or falling while walking?

- **More good days than bad** – Compare your Bengal's number of good days to bad, using a calendar or notepad if necessary.

Again, scores below 35 represent a diminished quality of life. However, if your Bengal's score is over 35, you may consider hospice or palliative care. As your Bengal ages, it's important to periodically evaluate his quality of life, especially if he suffers from a chronic illness. It can be devastating to think about the end of your time together, but it's important to have a plan in place.

The Euthanasia Process

Humane euthanasia is the most common way for a pet's life to end. Owners often opt for euthanasia to limit their animal's suffering and end its life as peacefully and pain-free as possible. The procedure is always performed by a licensed veterinarian. With the pet owner's consent, the veterinarian injects a lethal dose of sodium pentobarbital into the animal's bloodstream. Some vets will inject a mild sedative prior to euthanasia to help the animal relax, especially if it's nervous or frightened.

When you are ready to say goodbye to your Bengal, your veterinarian will begin by placing an IV catheter, usually on a front leg. The catheter makes it easier to inject the sedative and euthanasia solution and ensures that the procedure goes as smoothly as possible. Once the sedative has been administered, your veterinarian will likely wait a few minutes so that your cat can relax. Intravenous sedatives act quickly, so it won't take long for your Bengal to relax or fall asleep.

As with the sedative, sodium pentobarbital acts quickly, so once injected, the heart will begin to slow and eventually stop. The solution causes no discomfort, and the entire procedure usually lasts less than a minute. Your beloved Bengal will lose consciousness and peacefully drift away. Your veterinarian will then use a stethoscope to verify the moment that the heart stops beating.

Afterward, you will likely be given a few moments with your Bengal to say your final goodbyes. Veterinary staff are well-versed in grief, and they understand what you're going through. Most of them are pet owners as well, so they've been in the same place.

Final Arrangements

Making your Bengal's final arrangements can be incredibly difficult as you struggle with your grief. It's helpful to make plans long before you have to say goodbye. It can be a hard topic to discuss, but it's better to make arrangements when you are in a clear state of mind. Although you won't always know ahead of time, it's a good idea to have some plan in place that you can rely on when the time comes.

Chapter 15: When It's Time to Say Goodbye

Euthanasia is either performed in your home or at a veterinary clinic. Not all vets offer both options, so if you have a preference, you may need to find one that does. Some cats and owners become stressed in medical settings, while others would prefer not to have the event take place at home. Both options are valid, and your choice will depend on what works best for you and your family.

You will also need to decide whether you want to be present during the procedure. Many owners want to be with their beloved companions through their final moments, while others may not be able to handle seeing their pet pass. Your veterinarian may also allow you to pay beforehand so that you can leave immediately after saying goodbye.

As part of the final arrangements, you'll also need to decide what you want to do with your Bengal's remains. Most veterinary clinics are able to take care of the remains if you don't want to take them with you after the procedure. If cremation is your choice, you will also need to decide whether you want the ashes returned to you. Some clinics may also offer a variety of urns, but some may return the ashes in a simple cardboard box. Many online retailers and artisans offer a variety of beautiful urns if you choose to have your pet's ashes returned to you.

Grieving Your Loss

Grief is a unique and devastating experience. Anyone who has ever lost a loved one can understand the sorrow and emptiness. Many owners find the new silence of their home to be particularly upsetting. It's important to understand that grief is a normal human experience. You do not simply "get over" grief, but rather you grow with it. Your heart will never fill that hole but rather grow around it.

In 2018, researchers at the University of California and the University College Dublin performed a joint study to understand the experience of pet loss. They found that about half of all study participants experienced intense feelings of grief for between 12 and 19 months. Around 25% of the participants felt intense grief for 3 to 12 months, while the remaining 25% grieved for 12 to 24 months. You will not be able to rush through your grief overnight, so it's important to take your time in experiencing your feelings.

As you mourn the loss of your beloved Bengal, it's important to remember your happy times. Be grateful for every moment you shared. You can try sharing your memories or feelings in a journal or putting together a photo album of your favorite pictures. Many owners also work through their grief by preparing a memorial for their pets. Whether you choose to plant a tree, decorate a stone for your garden, or make a donation to a local rescue organization in your Bengal's name, consider the relationship you had with your companion and choose a memorial that you feel a connection to.

As stated earlier, if you've had your Bengal's ashes returned to you, you may choose to have a beautiful urn made. There are also a number of artists that can turn ashes into art or jewelry. The ashes can be incorporated into glass, ceramics, paint, and more. If you've saved any of your cat's hair, the artist may also be able to incorporate it into their work. Many artists are also able to make memorial sculptures made of wool, fabric, metal, or clay, all made in your pet's image.

The most important thing to remember during this difficult time is that you are not alone. The experience of losing a loved one is unique for everyone, but it's crucial that you do not isolate yourself. Being alone will only deepen your grief and damage your mental health. If others reach out to help you, try not to push them away. Your friends and family can support you through your time of need. If you do not have anyone close, you can also reach out to pet loss support groups. If you are having a difficult time grieving, you may also want to contact a mental health professional or grief counselor.

Saying goodbye to your beloved cat is one of the most difficult experiences you will have as a Bengal owner, but it's important to remember the unconditional love you shared with one another.